First World War
and Army of Occupation
War Diary
France, Belgium and Germany

35 DIVISION
Divisional Troops
Divisional Trench Mortar Batteries
1 July 1916 - 31 January 1919

WO95/2475/2

The Naval & Military Press Ltd
www.nmarchive.com
Published in association with The National Archives

Published by

The Naval & Military Press Ltd

Unit 10 Ridgewood Industrial Park,

Uckfield, East Sussex,

TN22 5QE England

Tel: +44 (0) 1825 749494

www.naval-military-press.com

www.nmarchive.com

This diary has been reprinted in facsimile from the original. Any imperfections are inevitably reproduced and the quality may fall short of modern type and cartographic standards.

© Crown Copyright
Images reproduced by permission of The National Archives, London, England, 2015.

Contents

Document type	Place/Title	Date From	Date To
Heading	35th Division Divl Artillery. Trench Mortar Batteries. Jly 1916 Jan 1919		
Heading	35th Divisional Artillery. War Diary X/35 Trench Mortar Battery. 1st to 31st July 1916		
Heading	War Diary of X/35 Trench Mortar Battery from 1st July to 31st July 1916. (Volume 1).		
War Diary	Bailleul aux Cornailles	01/07/1916	02/07/1916
War Diary	Authieule	03/07/1916	04/07/1916
War Diary	Gezaincourt	05/07/1916	06/07/1916
War Diary	Thievres	07/07/1916	13/07/1916
War Diary	Bois De Tailles	14/07/1916	19/07/1916
War Diary	Bonfray Farm	20/07/1916	31/07/1916
Heading	35th Divisional Artillery. War Diary Y/35 Trench Mortar Battery. 1st to 31st July 1916		
Heading	War Diary of Y/35 Trench Mortar Battery from 1st July to 31st. July 1916. (Volume 1).		
War Diary	Bailleul aux Cornailles	01/07/1916	02/07/1916
War Diary	Authieule	03/07/1916	04/07/1916
War Diary	Gezaincourt	05/07/1916	06/07/1916
War Diary	Thievres	07/07/1916	13/07/1916
War Diary	Bois De Tailles.	14/07/1916	19/07/1916
War Diary	Bonfray Farm	20/07/1916	31/07/1916
Heading	35th Divisional Artillery. War Diary Z/35 Trench Mortar Battery. 1st to 31st July 1916		
Heading	War Diary of Z/35 Trench Mortar Battery from 1st July to 31st July 1916. (Volume 1).		
War Diary	Bailleul aux Cornailles	01/07/1916	02/07/1916
War Diary	Authieule	03/07/1916	04/07/1916
War Diary	Gezaincourt	05/07/1916	06/07/1916
War Diary	Thievres	07/07/1916	13/07/1916
War Diary	Bois De Tailles	14/07/1916	19/07/1916
War Diary	Bonfray Farm	20/07/1916	01/08/1916
War Diary	Bray	02/08/1916	02/08/1916
War Diary	Forked Tree	03/08/1916	13/08/1916
War Diary	Dernancourt	14/08/1916	23/08/1916
War Diary	Bonfray Farm	24/08/1916	29/08/1916
War Diary	Autheux	30/08/1916	30/08/1916
War Diary	Doullens	31/08/1916	31/08/1916
Heading	War Diary of Y/35 Trench Mortar Battery. From 1st August 1916 to 31st August 1916. (Volume 2).		
War Diary	Bonfray Farm	01/08/1916	01/08/1916
War Diary	Bray	02/08/1916	02/08/1916
War Diary	Forked Tree	03/08/1916	13/08/1916
War Diary	Dernancourt	14/08/1916	23/08/1916
War Diary	Bonfray Farm	24/08/1916	29/08/1916
War Diary	Autheux	30/08/1916	30/08/1916
War Diary	Doullens	31/08/1916	31/08/1916
Heading	War Diary of Z/35 Trench Mortar Battery. from 1st August to 31st August 1916. (Volume 2).		
War Diary	Bonfray Farm	01/08/1916	01/08/1916

War Diary	Bray	02/08/1916	02/08/1916
War Diary	Forked Tree	03/08/1916	13/08/1916
War Diary	Dernancourt	14/08/1916	23/08/1916
War Diary	Bonfray Farm	24/08/1916	29/08/1916
War Diary	Autheux	30/08/1916	30/08/1916
War Diary	Doullens	31/08/1916	31/08/1916
Heading	War Diary of V/35 Trench Mortar Battery. from 12th September to 30th September 1916. (Volume 1).		
War Diary	Arras	12/09/1916	12/09/1916
War Diary	Ligny St. Flochel	13/09/1916	20/09/1916
War Diary	Arras	21/09/1916	30/09/1916
Heading	War Diary of X/35 Trench Mortar Battery. from 1st September to 30th September 1916. (Volume 3).		
War Diary	Doullens	01/09/1916	01/09/1916
War Diary	Denier	02/09/1916	04/09/1916
War Diary	Agnez-Lez-Duisans	05/09/1916	09/09/1916
War Diary	Arras	10/09/1916	30/09/1916
Heading	War Diary of Y/35 Trench Mortar Battery. from 1st September to 30th September 1916. (Volume 3).		
War Diary	Doullens	01/09/1916	01/09/1916
War Diary	Denier	02/09/1916	04/09/1916
War Diary	Agnez-Les-Duisans	05/09/1916	09/09/1916
War Diary	Arras	10/09/1916	30/09/1916
Heading	War Diary of Z/35 Trench Mortar Battery. from 1st September to 30th September 1916. (Volume 3).		
War Diary	Doullens.	01/09/1916	01/09/1916
War Diary	Denier	02/09/1916	04/09/1916
War Diary	Agnez-Les-Duisans.	05/09/1916	09/09/1916
War Diary	Arras	10/09/1916	30/09/1916
Heading	War Diary of V/35 Trench Mortar Battery. from 1st October to 31st October 1916. (Volume 2).		
War Diary	Arras	01/11/1916	30/11/1916
War Diary		20/11/1916	20/11/1916
Heading	War Diary of X/35 Trench Mortar Battery. from 1st October to 31st October 1916. (Volume 4).		
War Diary	Arras	01/10/1916	31/10/1916
Heading	War Diary of Y/35 Trench Mortar Battery from 1st October to 31st October 1916. (Volume 4).		
War Diary	Arras	01/10/1916	31/10/1916
Heading	War Diary of Z/35 Trench Mortar Battery from 1st October to 31st October 1916. (Volume 5).		
War Diary	Arras	01/10/1916	31/10/1916
Heading	War Diary of V/35 Trench Mortar Battery from 1st November to 30th November 1916. (Volume 3).		
War Diary	Arras	01/10/1916	31/10/1916
Heading	War Diary of X/35 Trench Mortar Battery from 1st November to 30th November 1916 (Volume 5)		
War Diary	Arras	01/11/1916	30/11/1916
War Diary	Arras	20/11/1916	20/11/1916
Heading	War Diary of Y/35 Trench Mortar Battery from 1st November to 30th November 1916. (Volume 5).		
War Diary	Arras	01/11/1916	30/11/1916
War Diary	Arras	20/11/1916	20/11/1916
Heading	War Diary of Z/35 Trench Mortar Battery from 1st November to 30th November 1916. (Volume 4).		
War Diary	Arras	01/11/1916	30/11/1916

War Diary	Arras	20/11/1916	20/11/1916
Heading	War Diary of V/35 Trench Mortar Battery from 1st December to 31st December 1916. Vol 4		
War Diary	Arras	01/12/1916	26/12/1916
War Diary	Wanquetin	27/12/1916	27/12/1916
War Diary	Canettemont	28/12/1916	31/12/1916
Heading	War Diary of X/35 Trench Mortar Battery from 1st December to 31st December 1916. Vol 6		
War Diary	Arras	01/12/1916	31/12/1916
Heading	War Diary of Y/35 Trench Mortar Battery from 1st to 31st December 1916. Vol. 6		
War Diary	Arras	01/12/1916	26/12/1916
War Diary	Wanquetin	27/12/1916	27/12/1916
War Diary	Canettemont	28/12/1916	31/12/1916
Heading	War Diary of Z/35 Trench Mortar Battery. from 1st December to 31st December 1916. Vol 6		
War Diary	Arras	01/12/1916	26/12/1916
War Diary	Wanquetin	27/12/1916	27/12/1916
War Diary	Canettemont	28/12/1916	31/12/1916
Heading	War Diary of V/35 Trench Mortar Battery from 1st January to 31st January 1917. Vol 5		
War Diary	Canettemont	01/01/1917	05/01/1917
War Diary	Sericourt	06/01/1917	14/01/1917
War Diary	Arras	15/01/1917	31/01/1917
Heading	War Diary of X/35 Trench Mortar Battery from 1st January to 31st January 1917. Vol 7		
War Diary	Arras	01/01/1917	01/01/1917
War Diary	Canettemont	02/01/1917	05/01/1917
War Diary	Sericourt	06/01/1917	14/01/1917
War Diary	Arras	15/01/1917	31/01/1917
Heading	War Diary of Y/35 Trench Mortar Battery from 1st January to 31st January 1917. Vol 7		
War Diary	Canettemont	01/01/1917	05/01/1917
War Diary	Sericourt	06/01/1917	14/01/1917
War Diary	Arras	15/01/1917	31/01/1917
Heading	War Diary of Z/35 Trench Mortar Battery from 1st January to 31st January 1917. Vol 17		
War Diary	Canettemont	01/01/1917	05/01/1917
War Diary	Sericourt	06/01/1917	14/01/1917
War Diary	Arras	15/01/1917	31/01/1917
Heading	War Diary of V/35 Trench Mortar Battery from 1st Feburary to 28th Feburary 1917. Vol 6		
War Diary	Arras	01/02/1917	05/02/1917
War Diary	Roziere	06/02/1917	07/02/1917
War Diary	Hardinval	08/02/1917	08/02/1917
War Diary	Bourdon	09/02/1917	17/02/1917
War Diary	St. Sauveur	18/02/1917	18/02/1917
War Diary	Aubigny	19/02/1917	19/02/1917
War Diary	Hangard	20/02/1917	20/02/1917
War Diary	Ignaucourt	21/02/1917	27/02/1917
War Diary	Rosieres	28/02/1917	28/02/1917
Heading	War Diary of X/35 Trench Mortar Battery from 1st February to 28th February 1917. Vol 8		
War Diary	Arras	01/02/1917	05/02/1917
War Diary	Roziere	06/02/1917	07/02/1917
War Diary	Hardinval	08/02/1917	08/02/1917

War Diary	Bourdon	09/02/1917	17/02/1917
War Diary	St. Sauveur	18/02/1917	18/02/1917
War Diary	Aubigny	19/02/1917	19/02/1917
War Diary	Hangard	20/02/1917	20/02/1917
War Diary	Ignaucourt	21/02/1917	27/02/1917
War Diary	Rosieres	28/02/1917	28/02/1917
Heading	War Diary of Y/35 Trench Mortar Battery from 1st February to 28th February 1917. Vol 8		
War Diary	Arras	01/02/1917	05/02/1917
War Diary	Roziere	06/02/1917	07/02/1917
War Diary	Hardinval	08/02/1917	08/02/1917
War Diary	Bourdon	09/02/1917	17/02/1917
War Diary	St. Sauveur	18/02/1917	18/02/1917
War Diary	Aubigny	19/02/1917	19/02/1917
War Diary	Hangard	20/02/1917	20/02/1917
War Diary	Ingaucourt	21/02/1917	27/02/1917
War Diary	Rosieres	28/02/1917	28/02/1917
Heading	War Diary of Z/35 Trench Mortar Battery from 1st February to 28th February 1917. Vol 8		
War Diary	Arras	01/02/1917	05/02/1917
War Diary	Roziere	06/02/1917	07/02/1917
War Diary	Hardinval	08/02/1917	08/02/1917
War Diary	Bourdon	09/02/1917	17/02/1917
War Diary	St. Sauveur	18/02/1917	18/02/1917
War Diary	Aubigny	19/02/1917	19/02/1917
War Diary	Hangard	20/02/1917	20/02/1917
War Diary	Ignaucourt	21/02/1917	27/02/1917
War Diary	Rosieres	28/02/1917	28/02/1917
Heading	War Diary of Y/35 Trench Mortar Battery from 1st March to 31st March 1917. Vol 7		
War Diary	Ignaucourt	01/03/1917	09/03/1917
War Diary	Rosieres	10/03/1917	16/03/1917
War Diary	Maucourt	17/03/1917	25/03/1917
War Diary	Warvillers	25/03/1917	25/03/1917
War Diary	Mesnil-St-Nicaise	26/03/1917	31/03/1917
Heading	War Diary of X/35 Trench Mortar Battery from 1st March to 31st March 1917. Vol 9		
War Diary		01/03/1917	31/03/1917
Heading	War Diary of Y/35 Trench Mortar Battery from 1st Mar to 31st March 1917. Vol. 9		
War Diary	Ignaucourt	01/03/1917	02/03/1917
War Diary	Rosieres	03/03/1917	14/03/1917
War Diary	Maucourt	15/03/1917	16/03/1917
War Diary	Chilly	17/03/1917	17/03/1917
War Diary	Maucourt	18/03/1917	25/03/1917
War Diary	Warvillers	26/03/1917	26/03/1917
War Diary	Mesnil-St-Nicaise	27/03/1917	31/03/1917
Heading	War Diary of Z/35 Trench Mortar Battery from 1st March to 31st March 1917. Vol 9		
War Diary	Ignaucourt	01/03/1917	01/03/1917
War Diary	Rosieres	11/03/1917	18/03/1917
War Diary	Maucourt	19/03/1917	25/03/1917
War Diary	Warvillers	26/03/1917	28/03/1917
War Diary	4th Army School of Mortar	29/03/1917	31/03/1917
Heading	War Diary of V/35 Trench Mortar Battery 1st April 1917 to 30th April 1917. Volume 8		

War Diary	Mesnil-St Nicaise	01/04/1917	14/04/1917
War Diary	Monchy-Lagache	15/04/1917	21/04/1917
War Diary	Monchy-Lagache	17/04/1917	25/04/1917
War Diary	Vermand	26/04/1917	30/04/1917
Heading	War Diary of X/35 Trench Mortar Battery from 1st April 1917 to 30th April 1917. Volume 10		
War Diary	Mesnil St Nicaise	01/04/1917	14/04/1917
War Diary	Monchy Lagache	03/04/1917	25/04/1917
War Diary	Vermand	26/04/1917	30/04/1917
Heading	War Diary of Y/35 Trench Mortar Battery from 1st April 1917 to 30th April 1917. Volume 10		
War Diary	Mesnil St Nicaise	01/04/1917	14/04/1917
War Diary	Monchy Lagache	15/04/1917	25/04/1917
War Diary	Vermand	26/04/1917	30/04/1917
Heading	War Diary of Z/35 Trench Mortar Battery from 1st April 1917 to 30th April 1917. Volume 10		
War Diary	Vaux-En-Amienois	01/04/1917	08/04/1917
War Diary	Mesnil-St-Nicaisse	09/04/1917	14/04/1917
War Diary	Monchy-Lagache	15/04/1917	25/04/1917
War Diary	Vermand	26/04/1917	30/04/1917
Miscellaneous	IV Corps. Report on Z/35 Trench Mortar Battery. Appendix 1		
Heading	War Diary of V/35 Trench Mortar Battery from 1st May 1917 to 31st May. 1917. (Volume 9).		
War Diary	Vermand	01/05/1917	21/05/1917
War Diary	Monchy-Lagache	22/05/1917	22/05/1917
War Diary	Doingt	23/05/1917	24/05/1917
War Diary	Vaux-En-Amienois	25/05/1917	31/05/1917
Heading	War Diary of X/35 Trench Mortar Battery from 1st May 1917 to 31st May 1917. Volume 11		
War Diary	Vermand	01/05/1917	21/05/1917
War Diary	Monchy-Lagache	22/05/1917	22/05/1917
War Diary	Peronne	23/05/1917	23/05/1917
War Diary	D.9 Central Sht. 62c	22/05/1917	31/05/1917
Heading	War Diary of Y/35 Trench Mortar Battery from 1st May 1917 to 31st May 1917. (Volume 11).		
War Diary	Vermand	01/05/1917	10/05/1917
War Diary	Vaux-En-Amienois	11/05/1917	24/05/1917
War Diary	Peronne	25/05/1917	26/05/1917
War Diary	D.9. Central Sht. 62.c.	27/05/1917	31/05/1917
Heading	War Diary of Z/35 Trench Mortar Battery from 1st May 1917 to 31st May 1917. (Volume 11).		
War Diary	Vermand	01/05/1917	21/05/1917
War Diary	Monchy-Lagache	22/05/1917	22/05/1917
War Diary	Peronne	23/05/1917	23/05/1917
War Diary	D.9. Central Sheet 62c.	24/05/1917	31/05/1917
Heading	War Diary of V/35 Trench Mortar Battery from 1st June 1917 to 30th June 1917. Volume 10		
War Diary	Vaux-En-Amienois	01/06/1917	05/06/1917
War Diary	Quinconce	06/06/1917	06/06/1917
War Diary	D.9. Central Sheet 62c.	07/06/1917	30/06/1917
Heading	War Diary of X/35 Trench Mortar Battery from 1st June 1917 to 30th June 1917. Volume 12		
War Diary	Nurlu	01/06/1917	07/06/1917
War Diary	Vaux-En-Amiennois	08/06/1917	18/06/1917
War Diary	Peronne	19/06/1917	19/06/1917

War Diary	Ronssoy	20/06/1917	30/06/1917
Heading	War Diary of Y/35 Trench Mortar Battery from 1st June 1917 to 30th June 1917. Volume 12		
War Diary	D.9. Central Sheet 62.c.	01/06/1917	08/06/1917
War Diary	X.13.a Sheet 57c. S.E.	09/06/1917	30/06/1917
Heading	War Diary of Z/35 Trench Mortar Battery from 1st June 1917 to 30th June 1917. Volume 12		
War Diary	Nurlu	01/06/1917	29/06/1917
War Diary	Ronssoy	30/06/1917	30/06/1917
Heading	War Diary of V/35 Trench Mortar Battery from 1st July 1917 to 31st July 1917. (Volume 11).		
War Diary	D.9. Central Sheet 62c.	01/07/1917	01/07/1917
War Diary	E.18.c.80.50. Sht 62c.	02/07/1917	04/07/1917
War Diary	Driencourt	05/07/1917	11/07/1917
War Diary	E.18.c.80.50. Sheet 62c.	12/07/1917	31/07/1917
Heading	War Diary of X/35 Trench Mortar Battery from 1st July 1917 to 31st July 17. (Volume 13).		
War Diary	Ronssoy	01/07/1917	04/07/1917
War Diary	St Emilie	05/07/1917	31/07/1917
Heading	War Diary of Y/35 Trench Mortar Battery from 1st July 17 to 31st July 17. (Volume 13).		
War Diary	D.9. Central Sheet 62c	01/07/1917	01/07/1917
War Diary	E.18.c.80.50 Sheet 62c	02/07/1917	31/07/1917
Heading	War Diary of Z/35 Trench Mortar Battery from 1st July 17 to 31st July 17. (Volume 13).		
War Diary	Ronssoy	01/07/1917	05/07/1917
War Diary	St. Emilie	06/07/1917	31/07/1917
Heading	War Diary of V/35 Trench Mortar Battery from 1st Aug 17 to 31st Aug 17. Volume 12		
War Diary	E.18.c.80.50. Sheet 62c.	01/07/1917	25/07/1917
Heading	War Diary of X/35 Trench Mortar Battery from 1st Aug 17 to 31st Aug 17. Volume 14		
War Diary	E.18.c.80.50	26/07/1917	31/07/1917
Heading	War Diary of X/35 Trench Mortar Battery from 1st Aug 17 to 31st Aug 17. Volume 14		
War Diary	E.18.c.80.50 Sheet 62c	01/08/1917	31/08/1917
Heading	War Diary of Y/35 Trench Mortar Battery from 1st Aug 17 to 31st Aug 17. Volume 14		
War Diary	Sheet 62c E.18c.80.50	01/08/1917	31/08/1917
Heading	War Diary of Z/35 Trench Mortar Battery from 1st Aug 17 to 31st Aug 17. Volume 14		
War Diary	St Emile	01/08/1917	31/08/1917
Heading	War Diary of V/35 Trench Mortar Battery from 1st Sept 17 to 30th Sept 17. Volume 13		
War Diary	E.18.c.80.50. Sheet 62c	01/09/1917	30/09/1917
Heading	War Diary Of X/35 Trench Mortar Battery from 1st Sept. 17 to 30th Sept 17. Volume 15		
War Diary	E.18.c.80.50	01/09/1917	30/09/1917
Heading	War Diary of Y/35 Trench Mortar Battery from 1st Sept 17 to 30th Sept 17. Volume 15		
War Diary	E.18.c.80.50 Sheet 62c	01/09/1917	30/09/1917
Heading	War Diary of Z/35 Trench Mortar Battery from 1st Sept 17 to 30th Sept 17. Volume 15		
War Diary	E.18.c.80.50. Sheet 62c	01/09/1917	30/09/1917
Heading	War Diary of V/35 Trench Mortar Battery from 1st October 1917 to 31st Oct 1917. Volume 14		

War Diary	E.18.c.80.50 Sheet 62c.	01/10/1917	04/10/1917
War Diary	Avesnes-Le Comte	05/10/1917	13/10/1917
War Diary	Eringhem	14/10/1917	16/10/1917
War Diary	B.10.c.60.40. Sheet 28 Belgium.	17/10/1917	20/10/1917
War Diary	B.13.a.70.70. Sheet 28 Belgium.	21/10/1917	31/10/1917
Heading	War Diary of X/35 Trench Mortar Battery from 1st October 1917 to 31st October 1917. Volume 16		
War Diary	E.18.c.80.50. Sht 62c	01/10/1917	03/10/1917
War Diary	Avesnes-Le-Comte	04/10/1917	13/10/1917
War Diary	Eringhem	14/10/1917	16/10/1917
War Diary	B.10c.60.40. Sheet 28 Belgium.	17/10/1917	20/10/1917
War Diary	B.13.A.70.70. Sheet 28	21/10/1917	31/10/1917
Heading	War Diary of V/35 Trench Mortar Battery from 1st October 1917 to 31st October 1917. Volume 16		
War Diary	E.18c.80.50. Sheet 62c	01/10/1917	01/10/1917
War Diary	Peronne	02/10/1917	02/10/1917
War Diary	Avesnes-Le-Comte	03/10/1917	13/10/1917
War Diary	Eringhem	14/10/1917	16/10/1917
War Diary	B.10.c.60.40 Sheet 28 Belgium	17/10/1917	20/10/1917
War Diary	B.13.A.70.70 Sheet 28	21/10/1917	31/10/1917
Heading	War Diary of Z/35 Trench Mortar Battery from 1st Oct 1917 to 31st Oct 1917. Volume 16		
War Diary	E.18.c.80.50 Sheet 62c	01/10/1917	01/10/1917
War Diary	Peronne	02/10/1917	02/10/1917
War Diary	Avesnes Le-Comte	03/10/1917	13/10/1917
War Diary	Eringhem	14/10/1917	16/10/1917
War Diary	B.10.c.60.40 Sheet 28 Belgium	17/10/1917	20/10/1917
War Diary	B.13.A.70.70 Sheet 28	21/10/1917	31/10/1917
Heading	War Diary of V/35 Trench Mortar Battery from 1st Nov. 1917 to 30th Nov 1917. Volume 15		
War Diary	B.13.A.70.70. Sheet 28	01/10/1917	14/10/1917
War Diary	B.9.c.00.40. Sheet 28	15/10/1917	30/10/1917
Miscellaneous Heading	War Diary of X/35 Trench Mortar Battery from 1st Nov 17 to 30th Nov 17. Volume 17		
War Diary	B.13.a.70.70 Sheet 28	01/11/1917	14/11/1917
War Diary	B.9.c.00.40 Sheet 28	15/11/1917	19/11/1917
War Diary	Valheureux	20/11/1917	30/11/1917
Miscellaneous Heading	War Diary of Y/35 Trench Mortar Battery from 1st Nov 17 to 30th Nov 17. Volume 17		
War Diary	B.13.a.70.70 Sheet 28	01/11/1917	14/11/1917
War Diary	B.9.c.00.40. Sheet 28	15/11/1917	30/11/1917
Miscellaneous Heading	War Diary of Z/35 Trench Mortar Battery from 1st Nov 17 to 30th Nov 17. Volume 17		
War Diary	B.13.a.70.70. Sheet 28	01/11/1917	14/11/1917
War Diary	B.9.c.00.40. Sheet 28	15/11/1917	30/11/1917
Miscellaneous Heading	War Diary of V/35 Trench Mortar Battery From 1st Dec. 1917 to 31st Dec. 1917. Volume 16		
War Diary	B.9.c. 00.40. Sheet 28	01/12/1917	09/12/1917
War Diary	Pera Camp E.16.b.5.5. Sheet 27	10/12/1917	12/12/1917
War Diary	Ledringhem	13/12/1917	31/12/1917
Heading	War Diary of X/35 Trench Mortar Battery from 1st Dec 1917 to 31st Dec 1917. Volume 18		

War Diary	Valheureux	01/12/1917	13/12/1917
War Diary	Arneke	14/12/1917	14/12/1917
War Diary	Ledringhem	15/12/1917	31/12/1917
Heading	War Diary of Y/35 Trench Mortar Battery from 1st Dec 1917 to 31st Dec 1917. Volume 18		
War Diary	B.9.c.00.40 Sheet 28	01/12/1917	08/12/1917
War Diary	Pera Camp E.16.b.5.5. Sheet 27	09/12/1917	12/12/1917
War Diary	Ledringhem	13/12/1917	16/12/1917
War Diary	Vaux-En-Amienois	17/12/1917	31/12/1917
Miscellaneous Heading	War Diary of Z/35 Trench Mortar Battery from 1st Dec 1917 to 31st Dec 1917. Volume 18		
War Diary	B.9.c.00.40. Sheet 28	01/12/1917	09/12/1917
War Diary	Pera Camp E.16.b.5.5. Sheet 27	10/12/1917	12/12/1917
War Diary	Ledringhem	13/12/1917	31/12/1917
Heading	War Diary of V/35 Trench Mortar Battery from 1st Jany 1918 to 31st Jany 1918. Volume 17		
War Diary	Ledringhem	01/01/1918	09/01/1918
War Diary	Welshfarm	10/01/1918	13/01/1918
War Diary	C.15.B.2.6. Sheet 28	14/01/1918	31/01/1918
Heading	War Diary of X/35 Trench Mortar Battery. from 1st Jany 1918 to 31st Jany 1918. Volume 19		
War Diary	Ledringhem	01/01/1918	09/01/1918
War Diary	Welsh Farm	10/01/1917	13/01/1917
War Diary	B.28. Central Sheet 28	14/01/1917	16/01/1917
War Diary	C.15.B.2.6. Sheet 28	17/01/1917	31/01/1917
Heading	War Diary of Y/35 Trench Mortar Battery from 1st Jany 1918 to 31st Jany 1918. Volume 19		
War Diary	Ledringhem	01/01/1918	04/01/1918
War Diary	Vaux-En-Amienois	05/01/1918	20/01/1918
War Diary	C.15.b.2.6	21/01/1918	31/01/1918
Heading	War Diary of V/35 Trench Mortar Battery from 1st Feby 1918 to 28th Feby 1918. Volume 18		
War Diary	Kempton Park C.15.b.2.6. Sheet 28	01/02/1918	08/02/1918
Heading	War Diary of X/35 Trench Mortar Battery from 1st Feby 1918 to 28th Feby 1918. Volume 20		
War Diary	Kempton Park C.15.b.2.6. Sheet 28	01/02/1918	28/02/1918
Miscellaneous Heading	War Diary of Y/35 Trench Mortar Battery from 1st Feby 1918 to 28th Feby 1918. Volume 20		
War Diary	Kempton Park C.15.b.2.6. Sheet 28	01/02/1918	28/02/1918
Miscellaneous Heading	War Diary of Z/35 Trench Mortar Battery From 1st Feby 1918 to 28th Feby 1918. Volume 20		
War Diary	Kempton Park C.15.b.2.6. Sheet 28	01/02/1918	08/02/1918
Miscellaneous Heading	35th Div. War Diary X/35 Trench Mortar Battery. March 1918		
War Diary	Vaux-En-Amienois	01/01/1918	05/01/1918
War Diary	Ledringhem	06/01/1918	09/01/1918
War Diary	Welsh Farm	10/01/1918	13/01/1918
War Diary	B.28. Central Sheet 28	14/01/1918	17/01/1918
War Diary	C.15.b.2.6 Sheet 28	18/01/1918	31/01/1918
War Diary	C.15.b.7.7. Sheet 28 N.W.	01/03/1918	10/03/1918
War Diary	Canal-Bank	11/03/1918	14/03/1918
War Diary	Crombeke	15/03/1918	24/03/1918

War Diary	Chipilly	25/03/1918	25/03/1918
War Diary	Hennencourt	26/03/1918	26/03/1918
War Diary	Warloy	27/03/1918	29/03/1918
War Diary	C.13.a Sheet 62 D.	30/03/1918	31/03/1918
Heading	35th Div. Y/35 Trench Mortar Battery. March 1918		
Miscellaneous			
Heading	War Diary of Y/35 Trench Mortar Battery from 1st March 1918 to 31st March 1918. Volume 21		
War Diary	C.15.b.7.7. Sheet 28 N.W.	01/03/1918	10/03/1918
War Diary	Canal Bk	11/03/1918	14/03/1918
War Diary	Crombeke	15/03/1918	24/03/1918
War Diary	Chipilly	25/03/1918	25/03/1918
War Diary	Hennencourt	26/03/1918	26/03/1918
War Diary	Warloy	27/03/1918	29/03/1918
War Diary	C.13.a Sheet 62 D.	30/03/1918	31/03/1918
Heading	War Diary of X/35 Trench Mortar Battery from 1st April 1918-to 30th April 1918. Volume 22		
War Diary	C.13 Central Sheet 62d	01/04/1918	01/04/1918
War Diary	Pont Noyelles	02/04/1918	06/04/1918
War Diary	Bresle	07/04/1918	11/04/1918
War Diary	Pont Noyelles	12/04/1918	12/04/1918
War Diary	Herrisart	13/04/1918	13/04/1918
War Diary	Warloy	14/04/1918	19/04/1918
War Diary	Senlis	20/04/1918	26/04/1918
War Diary	V.1.c.2.2	27/04/1918	30/04/1918
Heading	War Diary of Y/35. Trench Mortar Battery from 1st April 1918 to 31st. April 1918. Volume 22		
War Diary	Bresle	01/04/1918	06/04/1918
War Diary	Pont Noyelles	07/04/1918	11/04/1918
War Diary	Herrisart	12/04/1918	12/04/1918
War Diary	Senlis	13/04/1918	19/04/1918
War Diary	Warloy	20/04/1918	26/04/1918
War Diary	Senlis	27/04/1918	30/04/1918
Heading	War Diary of X/35 Trench Mortar Battery from 1st May 1918 to 31st May 1918. Volume 23		
War Diary	V.1.c.2.2. Sheet 57 D.	01/05/1918	03/05/1918
War Diary	Senlis	04/05/1918	09/05/1918
War Diary	V.1.c.2.2. Sheet 57d	10/05/1918	13/05/1918
War Diary	Senlis	14/05/1918	21/05/1918
War Diary	V.1.c.2.2	21/05/1918	25/05/1918
War Diary	Senlis	26/05/1918	31/05/1918
Miscellaneous			
Heading	War Diary of Y/35 Trench Mortar Battery from 1st May 1918 to 31st May 1918. Volume 23		
War Diary	Senlis	01/05/1918	04/05/1918
War Diary	V.1.c.2.2. Sheet 57 D.	05/05/1918	08/05/1918
War Diary	Senlis	09/05/1918	10/05/1918
War Diary	V.1.c.2.2	11/05/1918	19/05/1918
War Diary	Senlis	20/05/1918	25/05/1918
War Diary	V.1.c.2.2	26/03/1918	26/03/1918
War Diary	V.1.c.2.2. Sheet 57 D.	27/03/1918	31/03/1918
Miscellaneous			
Heading	War Diary of X/35 Trench Mortar Battery from 1st June 1918 to 30th June 1918. Volume 24		
Miscellaneous			
War Diary	Senlis	01/06/1918	02/06/1918

War Diary	V.18.d.9.1. Sheet 57 d	03/06/1918	07/06/1918
War Diary	Senlis	08/06/1918	13/06/1918
War Diary	V.18.d.9.1. (Sheet 57 d)	14/06/1918	16/06/1918
War Diary	Raincheval	17/06/1918	30/06/1918
Miscellaneous Heading	War Diary of Y/35 Trench Mortar Battery from 1st June 1918 to 30th June 1918. Volume 24		
War Diary	V.1.c.2.2. Sheet 57 D	01/06/1918	02/06/1918
War Diary	Senlis	03/06/1918	07/06/1918
War Diary	V.18.d.9.1. Sheet 57d	08/06/1918	12/06/1918
War Diary	Senlis	13/06/1918	16/06/1918
War Diary	Raincheval	17/06/1918	30/06/1918
Miscellaneous Heading	War Diary of Y/35 Trench Mortar Battery from 1st July 1918 to 31st July 1918. Volume 23		
War Diary	Raincheval	01/07/1918	02/07/1918
War Diary	Sheet 27 J.1.c.2.8	03/07/1918	07/07/1918
War Diary	Sheet 27 R.7.a.9.9	08/07/1918	31/07/1918
Miscellaneous Heading	War Diary of X/35 Trench Mortar Battery from 1st July 1918 to 31st July 1918. Volume 25		
War Diary	Raincheval	01/07/1918	02/07/1918
War Diary	Sheet 27 J.1.c.2.8	03/07/1918	07/07/1918
War Diary	Sheet 27 R.7.a.9.9	08/07/1918	31/07/1918
Miscellaneous Heading	War Diary of X/35 Trench Mortar Battery. from 1st August to 31st August 1918. Volume 26		
Miscellaneous			
War Diary	Sheet 27 R.7.a.9.9	01/08/1918	11/08/1918
War Diary	Sheet 27 R.21.a.10.80	12/08/1918	31/08/1918
Miscellaneous Heading	War Diary of Y/35. Trench Mortar Battery from 1st August to 31st August 1918. Volume 26		
Miscellaneous			
War Diary	Sheet 27 R.7.a.9.9	01/08/1918	31/08/1918
Miscellaneous Heading	War Diary of X/35 Trench Mortar Battery. from 1st Sept. 1918 to 30th Sept. 1918. Volume 27		
Miscellaneous			
War Diary	Sheet 27 E.10.a.5.4	01/09/1918	05/09/1918
War Diary	Sheet 28 H.7.c.7.4	06/09/1918	29/09/1918
War Diary	H.24.c.7.5	30/09/1918	30/09/1918
Miscellaneous Heading	War Diary of Y/35 Trench Mortar Battery from 1st Sept 1918 to 30th. Sept. 1918. Volume 27		
Miscellaneous			
War Diary	Sheet 27 E.10.a.5.4	01/09/1918	05/09/1918
War Diary	Sheet 28 H.7.c.7.4	06/09/1918	29/09/1918
War Diary	H.24.c.7.5	30/09/1918	30/09/1918
Miscellaneous Heading	War Diary of X/35 Trench Mortar Battery from 1st Octo to 31st Octo 1918. Volume 28		
Miscellaneous			
War Diary	Sheet 28 H.24.b.7.5	01/10/1918	19/10/1918
War Diary	Bisseghem	20/10/1918	26/10/1918
War Diary	Sweveghem	27/10/1918	27/10/1918

War Diary	O.2.b.8.3 Sheet 29		28/10/1918	31/10/1918
Miscellaneous				
Heading	War Diary of X/35 Trench Mortar Battery from 1st Octo to 31st Octo 1918. Volume 28			
Miscellaneous				
War Diary	Sheet 28 H.24.b.7.5		01/10/1918	14/10/1918
War Diary	Sheet 28 L.14.c.7.5		17/10/1918	22/10/1918
War Diary	Bisseghem		23/10/1918	26/10/1918
War Diary	Sweveghem		27/10/1918	31/10/1918
Miscellaneous				
Heading	War Diary of X/35 Trench Mortar Battery from 1st. Nov. 1918 to 30th Nov 1918. Volume 29			
Miscellaneous				
War Diary	Sheet 29 O.2.b.8.3		01/11/1918	08/11/1918
War Diary	Sheet 29 P.3.A.9.7		09/11/1918	09/11/1918
War Diary	X.4.c.6.4		10/11/1918	10/11/1918
War Diary	R.33.a.8.9		11/11/1918	12/11/1918
War Diary	Q.24.a.5.5		13/11/1918	13/11/1918
War Diary	Berchem		14/11/1918	16/11/1918
War Diary	Cuerne		17/11/1918	29/11/1918
War Diary	Menin		30/11/1918	30/11/1918
Miscellaneous				
Heading	War Diary of Y/35 Trench Mortar Battery from 1st Nov 1918 to 30th Nov. 1918. Volume 29			
Miscellaneous				
War Diary	Sheet 29 O.2.b.8.3		01/11/1918	08/11/1918
War Diary	Sheet 29 P.10.c.6.5		09/11/1918	09/11/1918
War Diary	Audenhove		10/11/1918	10/11/1918
War Diary	Sheet 30 O.31.d.6.0		11/11/1918	11/11/1918
War Diary	Sheet 29 R.33.a.8.9		12/11/1918	12/11/1918
War Diary	Sheet 29 Q.24.a.5.5		13/11/1918	13/11/1918
War Diary	Sheet 29 Q.21.b.		14/11/1918	16/11/1918
War Diary	Cuerne		17/11/1918	29/11/1918
War Diary	Menin		30/11/1918	30/11/1918
Miscellaneous				
Heading	War Diary of X/35 Trench Mortar Battery. from 1st Dec. 1918 to 31st Dec. 1918. Volume 30			
Miscellaneous				
War Diary	Poperinghe		01/12/1918	01/12/1918
War Diary	Terdeghem		02/12/1918	02/12/1918
War Diary	Nieurlet		03/12/1918	04/12/1918
War Diary	St Momelin		05/12/1918	30/12/1918
Miscellaneous				
Heading	War Diary of Y/35 Trench Mortar Battery. from 1st Dec. 1918 to 31st Dec. 1918. Volume 30			
Miscellaneous				
War Diary	Poperinghe		01/12/1918	01/12/1918
War Diary	Terdeghem		02/12/1918	02/12/1918
War Diary	Nieurlet		03/12/1918	04/12/1918
War Diary	St. Momelin		05/12/1918	30/12/1918
Miscellaneous				
Heading	War Diary of X/35 Trench Mortar Battery from 1st Jan 1919 to 31st Jan 1919. Volume 31			
Miscellaneous				
War Diary	St. Momelin		01/01/1919	31/01/1919
Miscellaneous				

Heading	War Diary Y/35 Trench Mortar Battery from 1st Jan 1919 to 31st Jan 1919 Volume 31		
Miscellaneous			
War Diary	St. Momelin	01/01/1919	31/01/1919
War Diary			

35TH DIVISION
DIVL ARTILLERY

TRENCH MORTAR BATTERIES
JU~~MAY~~ 1916 - JAN 1919

35TH DIVISION
DIVL ARTILLERY

35th Divisional Artillery

WAR DIARY

X /35 TRENCH MORTAR BATTERY

1st to 31st July 1916.

SECRET.

Vol 1

"War Diary
of
X/35 Trench Mortar Battery.
From 1st July to 31st July 1916.
(Volume 1)

P.M. Leckie 2nd Lt
Commanding X/35 T.M. Battery.

Army Form C. 2118.

WAR DIARY
INTELLIGENCE SUMMARY.
(Erase heading not required.)

X/35 TRENCH MORTAR BATTERY.

Instructions regarding War Diaries and Intelligence Summaries are contained in F.S. Regs, Part II. and the Staff Manual respectively. Title pages will be prepared in manuscript.

JULY, 1916.

Place	Date	Hour	Summary of Events and Information	Remarks and references to Appendices
BAILLEUL aux CORNAILLES	1		In billets at BAILLEUL aux CORNAILLES.	
"	2		Nothing to report.	
AUTHIEULE	3		Moved to AUTHIEULE.	
"	4		Nothing to report.	
GEZAINCOURT	5		Moved to GEZAINCOURT.	
"	6		Nothing to report.	
THIEVRES	7		Moved to THIEVRES.	
"	8-13		Nothing to report.	
BOIS DE TAILLES	14		Moved to BOIS DE TAILLES.	
"	15-19		Nothing to report.	
BONFRAY FARM	20		Moved to BONFRAY FARM.	
"	21-31		Nothing to report.	

CMLeckie 2nd Lt
Commanding X/35 Trench Mortar Battery.

35th Divisional Artillery

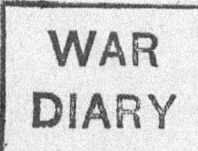

Y / 35 TRENCH MORTAR BATTERY

1st to 31st JULY 1916.

Secret

War Diary
of
Y/35 Trench Mortar Battery
From 1st July to 31st July 1916.
(Volume 1)

C.W.Thetford Lt R.F.A.
Commanding Y/35 T.M.Battery

Army Form C. 2118.

WAR DIARY
INTELLIGENCE SUMMARY.

(Erase heading not required.)

V/35 TRENCH MORTAR BATTERY

JULY, 1916.

Instructions regarding War Diaries and Intelligence Summaries are contained in F. S. Regs., Part II. and the Staff Manual respectively. Title pages will be prepared in manuscript.

Place	Date	Hour	Summary of Events and Information	Remarks and references to Appendices
BAILLEUL aux CORNAILLES.	1		In billets at BAILLEUL aux CORNAILLES.	
"	2		Nothing to report.	
AUTHIEULE	3		Moved to AUTHIEULE.	
"	4		Nothing to report.	
GEZAINCOURT	5		Moved to GEZAINCOURT.	
"	6		Nothing to report.	
THIEVRES	7		Moved to THIEVRES.	
"	8-13		Nothing to report.	
BOIS DE TAILLES.	14		Moved to BOIS DE TAILLES.	
"	15-19		Nothing to report.	
BONFRAY FARM	20		Moved to BONFRAY FARM.	
"	21-31		Nothing to report.	

Bohupos L.R.H
Commanding V/35 Trench Mortar Battery.

35th Divisional Artillery

WAR DIARY

Z / 35 TRENCH MORTAR BATTERY

1st to 31st JULY 1916.

SECRET.

"War Diary
of
Z/35 Trench Mortar Battery
from 1st July to 31st July 1916.
(Volume 1)

R Spalding
Lieut.
Commanding Z/35 T.M. Battery

Army Form C. 2118.

WAR DIARY
or
INTELLIGENCE SUMMARY.
(Erase heading not required.)

Z/35 TRENCH MORTAR BATTERY.   JULY 1916.

Instructions regarding War Diaries and Intelligence Summaries are contained in F. S. Regs., Part II. and the Staff Manual respectively. Title pages will be prepared in manuscript.

Place	Date	Hour	Summary of Events and Information	Remarks and references to Appendices
BAILLEUL aux CORNAILLES	1		In billets at BAILLEUL aux CORNAILLES.	
AUTHIEULE "	2		Nothing to report.	
"	3		Moved to AUTHIEULE.	
"	4		Nothing to report.	
GEZAINCOURT "	5		Moved to GEZAINCOURT.	
"	6		Nothing to report.	
THIEVRES "	7		Moved to THIEVRES.	
"	8-13		Nothing to report.	
BOIS DE TAILLES.	14		Moved to BOIS DE TAILLES.	
"	15-19		Nothing to report.	
BONFRAY FARM	20		Moved to BONFRAY FARM.	
"	21-31		Nothing to report.	

B. Spacey Lieut.
Commanding Z/35 Trench Mortar Battery.

Army Form C. 2118.

WAR DIARY
or
INTELLIGENCE SUMMARY.
(Erase heading not required.)

X/35 TRENCH MORTAR BATTERY

AUGUST, 1916.

Instructions regarding War Diaries and Intelligence Summaries are contained in F. S. Regs., Part II. and the Staff Manual respectively. Title pages will be prepared in manuscript.

Place	Date	Hour	Summary of Events and Information	Remarks and references to Appendices
BONFRAY FARM	1		At BONFRAY FARM.	OWL
BRAY	2		Moved to 1 mile N.W. of BRAY.	OWL
FORKED TREE	3		Moved to FORKED TREE. Started work on Ammunition dump.	OWL
" "	4-13		Working on Ammunition dump.	OWL
DERNANCOURT	14		Moved to DERNANCOURT.	OWL
"	15-20		Nothing to report.	OWL
"	21		Attached to No.1 Section D.A.C. for administrative purposes (including discipline).	OWL
"	22-23		Nothing to report.	OWL
BONFRAY FARM	24		Moved to BONFRAY FARM.	OWL
" "	25-29		Nothing to report.	OWL
AUTHEUX	30		Moved to AUTHEUX.	OWL
DOULLENS	31		Moved to DOULLENS.	OWL

OWLeckie 2nd Lt
Commanding X/35 Trench Mortar Battery.

Secret.

War Diary
of.
Y/35 Trench Mortar Battery.
From 1st August 1916 to 31st August 1916.
(Volume 2)

CW Pulford Lt. RFA.
Commanding Y/35 T.M. Battery.

Army Form C. 2118.

Y/35 TRENCH MORTAR BATTERY.

WAR DIARY
or
INTELLIGENCE SUMMARY.
(Erase heading not required.)

AUGUST, 1916.

Instructions regarding War Diaries and Intelligence Summaries are contained in F. S. Regs., Part II. and the Staff Manual respectively. Title pages will be prepared in manuscript.

Place	Date	Hour	Summary of Events and Information	Remarks and references to Appendices
BONFRAY FARM	1		At BONFRAY FARM.	
BRAY	2		Moved to 1 mile N.W. of BRAY.	
FORKED TREE	3		Moved to FORKED TREE. Started work on Ammunition dump.	
"	4-13		Working on Ammunition dump.	
DERNANCOURT	14		Moved to DERNANCOURT.	
"	15-20		Nothing to report.	
"	21		Attached to No.2 Section D.A.C. for administrative purposes (including discipline).	
"	22-23		Nothing to report.	
BONFRAY FARM	24		Moved to BONFRAY FARM.	
"	25-29		Nothing to report.	
AUTHEUX	30		Moved to AUTHEUX.	
DOULLENS	31		Moved to DOULLENS.	

Commanding Y/35 Trench Mortar Battery.

SECRET.

War Diary
of
Z/35 Trench Mortar Battery
From 1st August to 31st August 1916.
(Volume 2)

R. Spalding Lieut-
Commanding Z/35 T.M. Battery.

Army Form C. 2118.

WAR DIARY
INTELLIGENCE SUMMARY.
(Erase heading not required.)

Z/35 TRENCH MORTAR BATTERY   AUGUST, 1916.

Instructions regarding War Diaries and Intelligence Summaries are contained in F. S. Regs., Part II. and the Staff Manual respectively. Title pages will be prepared in manuscript.

Place	Date	Hour	Summary of Events and Information	Remarks and references to Appendices
BONFRAY FARM	1		At BONFRAY FARM.	
BRAY	2		Moved to 1 mile N.W. of BRAY.	
FORKED TREE	3		Moved to FORKED TREE. Started work on Ammunition dump.	
"	4-12		Working on Ammunition dump at FORKED TREE.	
"	13		Temp. Lieut. A.C.DAVIDSON invalided out of Battery.	
DERNANCOURT	14		Moved to DERNANCOURT.	
"	15-20		Nothing to report.	
"	21		Attached to No.3 Section D?A.G. for administrative purposes including discipline.	
"	22-23		Nothing to report.	
BONFRAY FARM	24		Moved to BONFRAY FARM.	
"	25-29		Nothing to report.	
AUTHEUX	30		Moved to AUTHEUX.	
DOULIENS	31		Moved to DOULIENS.	

Commanding Z/35 Trench Mortar Battery.

SECRET.

"War Diary
of
V/35 Trench Mortar Battery.
From 1st/12th September to 30th September 1916.
(Volume 1)

H.E. Walter
Commanding V/35 T.M. Battery

Army Form C. 2118.

WAR DIARY
or
INTELLIGENCE SUMMARY.
(Erase heading not required.)

V/35 Trench Mortar Battery.

September, 1916.

Instructions regarding War Diaries and Intelligence Summaries are contained in F.S. Regs., Part II. and the Staff Manual respectively. Title pages will be prepared in manuscript.

Place	Date	Hour	Summary of Events and Information	Remarks and references to Appendices
ARRAS	12		V/35 formed as part of 35th Div. Arty. Went to Third Army Trench Mortar School of Instruction at LIGNY ST. FLOCHEL. Establishment as follows:- 1 Captain, 2 Subalterns, 1 Clerk, 3 Sergeants, 1 Fitter, 4 Corporals, 4 Bombardiers, 47 Gunners, 2 Orderlies, 1 Cook, 3 Batmen and 2 bicycles.	
LIGNY ST. FLOCHEL.	13-20		At School of Instruction. 3rd Army Trench Mortar School.	
ARRAS	21		Left School of Instruction. Proceeded to ARRAS.	
"	22-24		Nothing to report.	
"	25		Went into action at ARRAS and took over section of line held by 21st Division. under 35th D.A.	
"	26-30		In action at ARRAS under 35th Div. Arty.	

H. Walker

Commanding V/35 Trench Mortar Battery.

SECRET

Vol 3

War Diary
of.
X/35 Trench Mortar Battery
From 1st September to 30th September 1916.
(Volume 3)

P.M. Leckie 2nd Lt
Commanding X/35 T.M. Bty

Army Form C. 2118.

WAR DIARY
of
INTELLIGENCE SUMMARY.

September, 1916.

(Erase heading not required.)

X/35 Trench Mortar Battery.

Instructions regarding War Diaries and Intelligence Summaries are contained in F. S. Regs., Part II. and the Staff Manual respectively. Title pages will be prepared in manuscript.

Place	Date	Hour	Summary of Events and Information	Remarks and references to Appendices
DOULLENS	1		In billets at DOULLENS.	OWL
DENIER	2		Moved to DENIER.	OWL
"	3-4		Nothing to report.	OWL
AGNEZ-les-DUISANS	5		Moved to AGNEZ-les-DUISANS.	OWL
"	6-9		Nothing to report.	OWL
ARRAS	10		Moved to ARRAS. Went into action under 35th D.A. in ARRAS section, taking over from batteries of 21st D.A. in section of line held by 21st Division.	OWL
"	11		Detached from No. 1 Section D.A.C. and came under administrative orders of D.T.M.O.	OWL
"	12-30		In action.	OWL

Ritchie 2nd Lt
Commanding X/35 Trench Mortar Battery.

SECRET.

War Diary
of
Y/35 Trench Mortar Battery
From 1st September to 30th September 1916.
(Volume 3)

CW Thelford Lt. R.F.A.
Commanding Y/35 T.M. Battery

Army Form C. 2118.

WAR DIARY
or
INTELLIGENCE SUMMARY.
(Erase heading not required.)

Y/35 TRENCH MORTAR BATTERY SEPTEMBER, 1916.

Instructions regarding War Diaries and Intelligence Summaries are contained in F. S. Regs., Part II. and the Staff Manual respectively. Title pages will be prepared in manuscript.

Place	Date	Hour	Summary of Events and Information	Remarks and references to Appendices
DOULLENS.	1		In billets at DOULLENS.	
DENIER	2		Moved to DENIER.	
"	3-4		Nothing to report.	
AGNEZ-LES-DUISANS.	5		Moved to AGNEZ-LEZ-DUISANS.	
"	6-9		Nothing to report.	
ARRAS	10		Moved to ARRAS. Went into action, taking over section of line from 21st. Division.	
"	11		Detached from No.2 Section D.A.C. and came under administrative orders of D.T.M.O.	
"	12-30		In action.	

Commanding Y/35 Trench Mortar Battery.

SECRET.

War Diary
of.
Z/35 Trench Mortar Battery
From 1st September to 30th September 1916.
(Volume 3)

R Spalding Lieut.
Commanding Z/35. T.M.Bty.

Army Form C. 2118.

WAR DIARY
or
INTELLIGENCE SUMMARY.

Z/35 TRENCH MORTAR BATTERY   SEPTEMBER, 1916.

Instructions regarding War Diaries and Intelligence Summaries are contained in F. S. Regs., Part II. and the Staff Manual respectively. Title pages will be prepared in manuscript.

(Erase heading not required.)

Place	Date	Hour	Summary of Events and Information	Remarks and references to Appendices
DOULLENS.	1		In billets at DOULLENS.	Ref.
DENIER	2		Moved to DENIER.	Ref.
"	3-4		Nothing to report.	Ref.
AGNEZ-LES-DUISANS.	5		Moved to AGNEZ-LEZ-DUISANS.	Ref.
"	6-9		Nothing to report.	Ref.
ARRAS	10		Moved to ARRAS. Went into action, in ARRAS section, taking over from batteries of 21st D.A. taking over section of line from 21st Division.	Ref.
"	11		Detached from No.3 Section D.A.C. and came under administrative orders of D.T.M.O.	Ref.
"	12-30		In action.	

R Spencer Shand.

Commanding Z/35 Trench Mortar Battery.

SECRET.

War Diary
of
V/35 Trench Mortar Battery
From 1st October to 31st October 1916.
(Volume 2)

H.E. Waller
Commanding V/35 T.M. Battery.

Army Form C. 2118.

WAR DIARY
of
INTELLIGENCE SUMMARY.
(Erase heading not required.)

V/35 Trench Mortar Battery.

November, 1916.

Instructions regarding War Diaries and Intelligence Summaries are contained in F. S. Regs., Part II. and the Staff Manual respectively. Title pages will be prepared in manuscript.

Place	Date	Hour	Summary of Events and Information	Remarks and references to Appendices
ARRAS	1		In action at ARRAS under orders of 35th Div. Arty.	
"	"		" " " " " " " " "	
"	2-30 20		Capt. E.W.R. FitzGerald, Lancashire Fus., appointed D.T.M.O. vice Capt. W.H. Price, Sherwood Foresters	

H.E. Baker
Commanding V/35 Trench Mortar Battery.

SECRET.

Vol

War Diary
of
X/35 Trench Mortar Battery
From 1st October to 31st October 1916.

(Volume 4)

PM Leckie 2nd Lt
  Commanding X/35 T.M. Battery

Army Form C. 2118.

WAR DIARY
or
INTELLIGENCE SUMMARY.

(Erase heading not required.)

X/35 Trench Mortar Battery

Instructions regarding War Diaries and Intelligence Summaries are contained in F. S. Regs., Part II. and the Staff Manual respectively. Title pages will be prepared in manuscript.

October, 1916.

Place	Date	Hour	Summary of Events and Information	Remarks and references to Appendices
ARRAS	1		In action in ARRAS section.	OL
			Following Officers posted to D.A.C., but supernumerary to establishment and appointed to X/35:-	OL
			2nd Lieut. A.B. WHALEY, R.F.A., 2nd Lieut. H.M. HEADLEY, R.F.A. and 2nd Lieut. J.S. BUTCHART, R.F.A.	
"	2-14		In action.	OL
"	15		1 O.R. wounded.	OL
"	16-31		In action.	OL

M.Lickie 2nd Lt
Commanding X/35 Trench Mortar Battery.

SECRET.

War Diary
of
Y/35 Trench Mortar Battery
From 1st October to 31st October 1916
(Volume 4)

GWMulford Lt. R.F.A.
Commanding Y/35 T.M. Battery.

Army Form C. 2118.

Y/35 TRENCH MORTAR BATTERY

WAR DIARY
or
INTELLIGENCE SUMMARY.

OCTOBER, 1916.

(Erase heading not required.)

Instructions regarding War Diaries and Intelligence Summaries are contained in F. S. Regs., Part II. and the Staff Manual respectively. Title pages will be prepared in manuscript.

Place	Date	Hour	Summary of Events and Information	Remarks and references to Appendices
ARRAS	1		In action in ARRAS section. Following officers posted to D.A.C. but supernumerary to establishment and appointed to Y/35 T.M. Battery :- Lieut. P.R.LURCOTT, 24th London Regt., 2/Lieut. C.W.PULFORD, R.F.A.	
"	2-31		In action.	

[signature] Lt. R.F.A.
Commanding Y/35 Trench Mortar Battery.

SECRET.

War Diary

of

Z/35 Trench Mortar Battery

From 1st October to 31st October 1916.

(Volume 5)

R A Spalding Lt
Commanding Z/35 T.M. Battery.

Army Form C. 2118.

Z/35 TRENCH MORTAR BATTERY

WAR DIARY

INTELLIGENCE SUMMARY.

OCTOBER, 1916.

Instructions regarding War Diaries and Intelligence Summaries are contained in F.S. Regs., Part II. and the Staff Manual respectively. Title pages will be prepared in manuscript.

(Erase heading not required.)

Place	Date	Hour	Summary of Events and Information	Remarks and references to Appendices
ARRAS	1		In action in ARRAS Section. Following officers posted to D.A.C. but supernumerary to establishment and appointed to Z/35 T.M. Battery :- 2/Lieut. J.B.GUYER, R.G.A., 2/Lieut. G.G.D.SCOTT, R.F.A.	
"	2-20		In action.	
"	21		2/Lieut. J.B.GUYER promoted Temp. Lieut. while in command of battery.	
"	22-31		In action.	

R.S.Beaudry Lr.
Commanding Z/35 Trench Mortar Battery.

SECRET.

War Diary
of
V/35 Trench Mortar Battery
From 1st November to 30th November 1916.
(Volume 3)

H.E. Walker
Commanding V/35 T.M. Battery

Army Form C. 2118.

WAR DIARY
or
INTELLIGENCE SUMMARY.
(Erase heading not required.)

V/35 Trench Mortar Battery. October, 1916.

Place	Date	Hour	Summary of Events and Information	Remarks and references to Appendices
ARRAS	1		In action at ARRAS.	
			Following Officers posted to D.A.C., but supernumerary to establishment and appointed to V/35:-	
			2nd Lieut. E.A. LOWE, R.G.A. (in Command with rank of Temp. Capt.) Lieut. C.H. KILPATRICK, R.F.A. and 2nd Lieut. C.R. HARPER, R.F.A.	
"	2-31		In action at ARRAS under orders of 35th Div. Arty.	

H. Walker
Commanding V/35 Trench Mortar Battery.

SECRET.

War Diary

of

X/35 Trench Mortar Battery

from 1st November to 30th November 1916.

(Volume 5)

P.M. Leckie 2nd Lt
 Commanding X/35. T.M. Battery

Army Form C. 2118.

WAR DIARY
or
INTELLIGENCE SUMMARY.
(Erase heading not required.)

X/35 Trench Mortar Battery. November, 1916.

Instructions regarding War Diaries and Intelligence Summaries are contained in F. S. Regs., Part II. and the Staff Manual respectively. Title pages will be prepared in manuscript.

Place	Date	Hour	Summary of Events and Information	Remarks and references to Appendices
ARRAS	1		In action in ARRAS section.	O.K.
"	2-28		In action.	O.K.
"	29		2nd Lieut. H.M. HEADLEY, R.F.A. posted from X/35 to 157th Brigade, R.F.A.	O.K.
"	29		2nd Lieut. P.M. LECKIE, R.F.A. posted from 157th Brigade, R.F.A. to X/35.	O.K.
"	30		In action.	O.K.
"	20		Capt. E.W.R. Fitzgerald L.F. appointed D.T.M.O. vice Capt. W.H. Price, notts & Derby	O.K.

P.M. Leckie 2nd Lt
Commanding X/35 Trench Mortar Battery.

SECRET.

War Diary
of
Y/35 Trench Mortar Battery
From 1st November to 30th November 1916.

(Volume 5)

Rutherford Lt. R.F.A.
Commanding Y/35 T.M. Battery

Army Form C. 2118.

Y/35 TRENCH MORTAR BATTERY.

WAR DIARY
or
INTELLIGENCE SUMMARY.
(Erase heading not required.)

NOVEMBER, 1916.

Instructions regarding War Diaries and Intelligence Summaries are contained in F. S. Regs., Part II. and the Staff Manual respectively. Title pages will be prepared in manuscript.

Place	Date	Hour	Summary of Events and Information	Remarks and references to Appendices
ARRAS	1		In action in ARRAS Section.	
"	2	2-30	In action.	
"		20	Capt. E. W. R. Fitzgerald, R.E. appointed D.T.M.O., vice Capt. W. H. Price, Notts & Derby.	

E. W. Ackford / R.F.A.
Commanding Y/35 Trench Mortar Battery.

SECRET.

War Diary
of
Z/35 Trench Mortar Battery
From 1st November to 30th November 1916.
(Volume 4)

R H Spalding
Lieut.
Commanding Z/35. T.M. Battery.

Army Form C. 2118.

WAR DIARY
or
INTELLIGENCE SUMMARY.

(Erase heading not required.)

Z/35 TRENCH MORTAR BATTERY.   NOVEMBER, 1916.

Instructions regarding War Diaries and Intelligence Summaries are contained in F. S. Regs., Part II. and the Staff Manual respectively. Title pages will be prepared in manuscript.

Place	Date	Hour	Summary of Events and Information	Remarks and references to Appendices
ARRAS	1		In action in ARRAS Section.	
"	2-25		In action.	
"	26		2/Lieut. G.G.D. SCOTT, posted to 157th Brigade R.F.A.	
"	27-30		In action.	
"	20		Capt. E.W.R. Fitzgerald, L.F. appointed D.T.M.O. vie Capt. W.W. Price, R.O.B. & Duty.	

R. Spalding
Commanding Z/35 Trench Mortar Battery.

SECRET.

War Diary

of

V/35 Trench Mortar Battery.

From 1st December to 31st December 1916.

Vol. 4

HE Walker   Commanding V/35 Trench Mortar Battery

Army Form C. 2118.

V/35 Trench Mortar Battery.

Instructions regarding War Diaries and Intelligence Summaries are contained in F. S. Regs., Part II. and the Staff Manual respectively. Title pages will be prepared in manuscript.

WAR DIARY
INTELLIGENCE SUMMARY.
(Erase heading not required.)

DECEMBER, 1916.

Place	Date	Hour	Summary of Events and Information	Remarks and references to Appendices
ARRAS	1		In action in trenches held by 35th Division in ARRAS Sector. Hdqrs. of D.T.M.O. in ARRAS. MEW.	
"	2		Nothing to report. MEW.	
"	3		Nothing to report. MEW.	
"	4		Nothing to report. MEW.	
"	5		9th Division took over line held by 35th Div:- 35th D.A. remained in action. MEW. 2nd Lieut. C.R.HARPER struck off strength with effect from 17/11/16 (sick in England) MEW.	
"	6		Nothing to report. MEW.	
"	7-19		Nothing to report. MEW.	
"	20		Captain E.A.LOWE, R.G.A. struck off strength with effect from 15/12/16 on appointment as Instructor at Fourth Army T.M. School. MEW. Captain W.H.PRICE, 15th Sherwood Foresters to temporarily command V/35 T.M. Battery vice Capt. E.A.LOWE, R.G.A. with effect from 16/12/16. MEW. 2nd Lieut. H.M.MICHIE, 159th Brigade R.F.A. posted vice 2nd Lieut. C.R.HARPER with effect from 18/11/16. MEW.	
"	21		Nothing to report. MEW.	
"	22-26		T.M. Batteries of 9th D.A. relieved T.M. Batteries of 35th D.A.(less X/35 T.M.Bty.) in the line.	
WANQUETIN	27		Marched to WANQUETIN on relief. MEW.	
CANETTEMONT	28		Marched to CANETTEMONT. MEW.	
CANETTEMONT	29-31		Nothing to report. MEW.	

Ammn: Expenditure for month 95 rounds.

W.H.Price

Commanding V/35 T.M. Battery.

SECRET.

War Diary

of

X/35 Trench Mortar Battery

from 1st December to 31st December 1916

Vol. 6

P.N. Leckie 2nd Lt
R.F.A.
Commanding X/35 Trench Mortar Battery

Army Form C. 2118.

WAR DIARY
INTELLIGENCE SUMMARY.

X/35 Trench Mortar Battery.

DECEMBER, 1916.

Instructions regarding War Diaries and Intelligence Summaries are contained in F. S. Regs., Part II. and the Staff Manual respectively. Title pages will be prepared in manuscript.

(Erase heading not required.)

Place	Date	Hour	Summary of Events and Information	Remarks and references to Appendices
ARRAS	1		In action in trenches held by 35th Division in ARRAS Sector. Headquarters of D.T.M.O. in ARRAS.	ONL
"	2-4		Nothing to report.	ONL
"	5		9th Division took over line held by 35th Division. 35th D.A. remained in action.	ONL
"	6-26		Nothing to report.	ONL
"	27		X/35 came under orders of 9th Division on relief of 35th D.A. by 9th D.A.	ONL
"	28-31		Nothing to report.	

Ammn. Expenditure for month 972 rounds.

CH Leckie 2nd Lt
RFA
Commanding X/35 T.M. Battery.

SECRET.

War Diary

of

Y/35 Trench Mortar Battery

From 1st to 31st December 1916

Vol. 6

J. E. Whitcherch Lt.
Commanding Y/35 Trench Mortar Battery

Army Form C. 2118.

WAR DIARY

INTELLIGENCE SUMMARY.

Y/35 Trench Mortar Battery.

DECEMBER, 1916

Instructions regarding War Diaries and Intelligence Summaries are contained in F.S. Regs., Part II. and the Staff Manual respectively. Title pages will be prepared in manuscript.

(Erase heading not required.)

Place	Date	Hour	Summary of Events and Information	Remarks and references to Appendices
ARRAS	1		In action in trenches held by 35th Division in ARRAS Sector. Hdqrs. of D.T.M.O. in ARRAS.	
"	2-4		Nothing to report.	
"	5		9th Division took over line held by 35th Division. 35th D.A. remained in action.	
"	6-16		Nothing to report.	
"	17		Lieut. P.R.LURCOTT (24th London Regiment) struck off strength with effect from 13/12/16 (sick in England).	
"	18-20		Nothing to report.	
"	21		2nd Lieut. C.W.PULFORD, 159th Brigade R.F.A. to command Y/35 T.M. Bty. with Acting rank of Lieut. vice Lieut. P.R.LURCOTT with effect from 14/12/16.	
"	22-26		Nothing to report.	
WANQUETIN	27		T.M. Batteries of 9th D.A. relieved T.M. Batteries of 35th D.A. (less X/35 T.M.Bty.) in the line. Marched to WANQUETIN on relief.	
CANETTEMONT	28		Marched to CANETTEMONT.	
"	29-31		Nothing to report.	

Ammn. Expenditure for month 1092 rounds.

J.H.Whitham Lt.
Commanding Y/35 T.M. Battery.

SECRET.

1916

War Diary

of

Z/35 Trench Mortar Battery

from 1st December to 31st December. 1916.

Vol. 6

G. Waggett 2 Lt
for Commanding Z/35 Trench Mortar Battery

Army Form C. 2118.

Z/35 Trench Mortar Battery.

WAR DIARY
or
INTELLIGENCE SUMMARY.
(Erase heading not required.)

DECEMBER, 1916.

Instructions regarding War Diaries and Intelligence Summaries are contained in F.S. Regs., Part II. and the Staff Manual respectively. Title pages will be prepared in manuscript.

Place	Date	Hour	Summary of Events and Information	Remarks and references to Appendices
ARRAS	1		In action in trenches held by 35th Division in ARRAS Sector. Hdqrs. of D.T.M.O. in ARRAS.	
"	2-4		Nothing to report.	
"	5		9th Division took over line held by 35th Division. 35th D.A. remained in action.	
"	6-20		Nothing to report.	
"	21		2nd.Lieut. (Acting Lieut) J.B.GUYER, R.G.A. posted to 1/1st Lowland Heavy Battery, R.G.A. and struck off strength with effect from 21/12/16. 2nd.Lieut. J.B.GUYER relinquishes the Acting rank of Lieut. on ceasing to command a Medium T.M. Battery.	
"	22-26		Nothing to report.	
WANQUETIN.	27		T.M. Batteries of 9th D.A. relieved T.M. Batteries of 35th D.A. (less X/35 T.M. Bty) in the line. Marched to WANQUETIN on relief.	
CANETTEMONT	28		Marched to CANETTEMONT.	
"	29		2nd.Lieut. R.F.SPALDING, 19th D.L.I. to command Z/35 T.M. Battery with Acting rank of Lieut. vice 2nd.Lieut. J.B.GUYER, R.G.A. with effect from 22/12/16. 2nd.Lieut. J.D.TAGGART, 157th Brigade R.F.A. posted with effect from 28/12/16.	
"	30-31		Nothing to report.	

Ammn. Expenditure for month - 964 rounds.

[signature]
for Commanding Z/35 T.M. Battery.

SECRET.

War Diary
of
V/35 Trench Mortar Battery
from 1st January to 31st January, 1917.
Vol. 5.

H.E. Walter Commanding V/35 Trench Mortar Battery

Army Form C. 2118.

WAR DIARY
or
INTELLIGENCE SUMMARY.
(Erase heading not required.)

V/35 Trench Mortar Battery.

JANUARY, 1917.

Instructions regarding War Diaries and Intelligence Summaries are contained in F.S. Regs., Part II. and the Staff Manual respectively. Title pages will be prepared in manuscript.

Place	Date	Hour	Summary of Events and Information	Remarks and references to Appendices
CANETTEMONT	1		In Rest Billets. MR.	
"	2-5		Nothing to report. MR.	
SERICOURT	6		Moved to SERICOURT. MR.	
"	7		Nothing to report. MR.	
"	8		2nd. Lieut. H.E.WALLER, R.F.A. joined from 14th Division. MR.	
"	9-14		Nothing to report. MR.	
ARRAS	15		Moved to ARRAS. MR.	
"	16		Started work on construction of T.M. Emplacements in trenches held by 12th Division. MR.	firing over 2 g.45"T.M's a certain amt.
"	17-19		Nothing to report. MR.	
"	20		Divisional Commander approves of 2nd. Lieut. H.E.WALLER, R.F.A. wearing the badges of Captain whilst in command of V/35 T.M. Battery. MR.	
"	21-31		Nothing to report. MR.	

Ammn. Expenditure for month - 272 rounds.

HEWaller
Commanding V/35 T.M. Battery.

SECRET.

War Diary
of
X/35 Trench Mortar Battery
From 1st January to 31st January 1917.
Vol. 4

P McLeckie 2nd Lt
RFA.
Commanding X/35 Trench Mortar Battery

Army Form C. 2118.

X/35 Trench Mortar Battery.

WAR DIARY
INTELLIGENCE SUMMARY.
(Erase heading not required.)

JANUARY, 1917.

Instructions regarding War Diaries and Intelligence Summaries are contained in F.S. Regs., Part II. and the Staff Manual respectively. Title pages will be prepared in manuscript.

Place	Date	Hour	Summary of Events and Information	Remarks and references to Appendices
ARRAS	1		In action in ARRAS Sector under 9th Division.	ONL
CANETTEMONT	2		Withdrawn from action and joined remainder of 35th D.A., T.M. Batteries at CANETTEMONT.	ONL
"	3-5		Nothing to report.	ONL
SERICOURT	6		Moved to SERICOURT.	ONL
"	6-14		Nothing to report.	ONL
ARRAS	15		Moved to ARRAS.	ONL
"	16		Started work on construction of T.M. Emplacements in Trenches held by 12th Division.	ONL
"	17-22		Nothing to report.	ONL
"	23		Relieved Z/35 T.M. Battery in action in trenches held by 12th Division.	ONL
"	24-27		Nothing to report.	ONL
"	28		Withdrawn from action on relief by Y/35 T.M. Battery.	ONL
"	29-31		Nothing to report.	ONL

Ammunition Expenditure for month - 317 rounds

ORLeckie 2nd Lt
RFA   Commanding X/35 T.M. Battery.

SECRET

War Diary

of

Y/35 Trench Mortar Battery

From 1st January to 31st January, 1917.

Vol. 4

J. G. Whitley
Commanding Y/35 Trench Mortar Battery.

Army Form C. 2118.

WAR DIARY
or
INTELLIGENCE SUMMARY.

Y/35* Trench Mortar Battery.

JANUARY, 1917.

(Erase heading not required.)

Instructions regarding War Diaries and Intelligence Summaries are contained in F. S. Regs., Part II. and the Staff Manual respectively. Title pages will be prepared in manuscript.

Place	Date	Hour	Summary of Events and Information	Remarks and references to Appendices
CANETTEMONT	1		In Rest Billets.	
"	2-5		Nothing to report.	
SERICOURT	6		Moved to SERICOURT.	
"	7-14		Nothing to report.	
ARRAS	15		Moved to ARRAS and relieved Medium T.M. Battery of 9th Division in action in Sector held by Infantry of 12th Division.	
"	16-18		Nothing to report.	
"	19		Withdrawn from action on relief by Z/35 T.M. Battery. Concentrated in ARRAS for work on T.M. Emplacements.	
"	20		2nd. Lieut. C.W.PULFORD, Y/35 T.M. Battery to be Acting Lieut. whilst commanding a T.M. Bty. with effect from 14/12/16.	
"	21-27		Nothing to report.	
"	28		Relieved X/35 T.M. Battery in action in trenches held by 12th Division.	
"	29-31		Nothing to report.	

Ammn. Expenditure for month - 408 rounds

J.S.Whitehead. Lieut.
Commanding Y/35 T.M. Battery.

SECRET.

1917

War Diary
of
Z/35 Trench Mortar Battery
From 1st January to 31st January, 1917.
Vol. 4

Taggart 2/Lt
for Commanding Z/35 Trench Mortar Battery

Army Form C. 2118.

WAR DIARY
or
INTELLIGENCE SUMMARY.

Z/35 Trench Mortar Battery.

JANUARY, 1917.

(Erase heading not required.)

Place	Date	Hour	Summary of Events and Information	Remarks and references to Appendices
CANETTEMONT	1		In Rest Billets.	
"	2-5		Nothing to report.	
SERICOURT	6		Moved to SERICOURT.	
"	7-14		Nothing to report.	
ARRAS	15		Moved to ARRAS.	
"	16		Started work on construction of T.M. Emplacements in Trenches held by 12th Division.	
"	17-18		Nothing to report.	
"	19		Relieved Y/35 T.M. Battery in action in trenches held by 12th Division.	
"	20-22		Nothing to report.	
"	23		Withdrawn from action on relief by X/35 T.M. Battery.	
"	24-31		Nothing to report.	

Ammn. Expenditure for month – 284 rounds.

[signature]
for Commanding Z/35 T.M. Battery.

SECRET.

War Diary
of
V/35 Trench Mortar Battery
From 1st February to 28th February 1917.
Vol. 6

H.E.Walker   Commanding V/35 Trench Mortar Battery

Army Form C. 2118.

WAR DIARY
INTELLIGENCE SUMMARY.
(Erase heading not required.)

V/35 Trench Mortar Battery.

Instructions regarding War Diaries and Intelligence Summaries are contained in F.S. Regs., Part II. and the Staff Manual respectively. Title pages will be prepared in manuscript.

FEBRUARY, 1917.

Place	Date	Hour	Summary of Events and Information	Remarks and references to Appendices
ARRAS	1		Concentrated for work on T.M. emplacements in ARRAS Sector. MR.	(2 9.45" T.M's in action in Roeuches held by (2H. Sw.) MRu
"	2-4		Nothing to report. MR.	
"	5		Moved by motor lorry to ROZIERE after dusk. MR.	
ROZIERE	6-7		Nothing to report. MR.	
HARDINVAL	8		Moved to HARDINVAL. MR.	
BOURDON	9		Moved to BOURDON. MR.	
"	10-17		Nothing to report. MR.	
St. SAUVEUR	18		Moved to St. SAUVEUR. MR.	
AUBIGNY	19		Moved to AUBIGNY. MR.	
HANGARD	20		Moved to HANGARD. MR.	
IGNAUCOURT	21		Moved to IGNAUCOURT. MR.	
"	22-27		Nothing to report. MR.	
ROSIERES	28		Moved to ROSIERES, leaving rear parties at IGNAUCOURT. MR.	

Amm'n Expenditure for month — 104 rounds.

HEWaller
Commanding V/35 T.M. Battery.

SECRET

War Diary

of

X/35 Trench Mortar Battery

From 1st February to 28th February 1917.

Vol. 8.

P.M.Leckie 2nd Lt
RFA
Commanding X/35 Trench Mortar Battery

Army Form C. 2118.

X/35 Trench Mortar Battery.

Instructions regarding War Diaries and Intelligence Summaries are contained in F.S. Regs., Part II. and the Staff Manual respectively. Title pages will be prepared in manuscript.

WAR DIARY or INTELLIGENCE SUMMARY.

FEBRUARY, 1917.

(Erase heading not required.)

Place	Date	Hour	Summary of Events and Information	Remarks and references to Appendices
ARRAS	1		Concentrated for work on T.M. emplacements in ARRAS Sector.	Nil
"	2-4		Nothing to report.	Nil
"	5		Moved by motor lorry to ROZIERE after dusk.	Nil
ROZIERE	6-7		Nothing to report.	Nil
HARDINVAL	8		Moved to HARDINVAL.	Nil
BOURDON	9		Moved to BOURDON.	Nil
"	10-17		Nothing to report.	Nil
St.SAUVEUR	18		Moved to ST.SAUVEUR.	Nil
AUBIGNY	19		Moved to AUBIGNY.	Nil
HANGARD	20		Moved to HANGARD.	Nil
IGNAUCOURT	21		Moved to IGNAUCOURT.	Nil
"	22-27		Nothing to report.	
ROSIERES.	28		Moved to ROSIERES, leaving rear parties at IGNAUCOURT.	

McLeckie 2nd Lt
RFA Commanding X/35 T.M. Battery.

SECRET.

War Diary
of
Y/35 Trench Mortar Battery
from 1st February to 28th February 1917.
Vol. 8.

A. E. [illegible]
for Commanding Y/35 Trench Mortar Battery

Army Form C. 2118.

WAR DIARY
INTELLIGENCE SUMMARY.

(Erase heading not required.)

Y/35 Trench Mortar Battery.

Instructions regarding War Diaries and Intelligence Summaries are contained in F.S. Regs., Part II. and the Staff Manual respectively. Title pages will be prepared in manuscript.

FEBRUARY, 1917.

Place	Date	Hour	Summary of Events and Information	Remarks and references to Appendices
ARRAS	1		In action in ARRAS Sector under 35th D.A. in trenches held by Infantry of 12th Division.	
"	2-4		Nothing to report. Relieved by Z/35 during morning	
"	5		Withdrawn from Action ARRAS on relief by T.M. Batteries of 12th D.A. Moved by motor lorry to ROZIERE after dusk.	
ROZIERE	6-7		Nothing to report.	
HARDINVAL	8		Moved to HARDINVAL.	
BOURDON	9		Moved to BOURDON.	
"	10-17		Nothing to report.	
ST.SAUVEUR	18		Moved to ST.SAUVEUR.	
AUBIGNY	19		Moved to AUBIGNY.	
HANGARD	20		Moved to HANGARD.	
IGNAUCOURT	21		Moved to IGNAUCOURT.	
"	22-27		Nothing to report.	
ROSIERES	28		Moved to ROSIERES, leaving rear parties at IGNAUCOURT.	

Ammn. expenditure for month – nil.

J.Y. Whitches Lieut.
Commanding Y/35 T.M. Battery.

SECRET.

Vol 8

War Diary
of
Z/35 Trench Mortar Battery
From 1st February to 28th February 1917

Vol. 8

J.H. Taggart 2/Lt
Commanding Z/35 Trench Mortar Battery

Army Form C. 2118.

WAR DIARY
INTELLIGENCE SUMMARY.
(Erase heading not required.)

Z/35 Trench Mortar Battery.

FEBRUARY, 1917.

Instructions regarding War Diaries and Intelligence Summaries are contained in F.S. Regs., Part II. and the Staff Manual respectively. Title pages will be prepared in manuscript.

Place	Date	Hour	Summary of Events and Information	Remarks and references to Appendices
ARRAS	1		Concentrated for work on T.M. emplacements in ARRAS Sector. Relieved Y/35 in action during hours	
"	2		Casualties O.R. 1 killed and 1 wounded.	
"	3-4		Nothing to report.	
"	5		Moved to ROZIERE by motor lorry after dusk. Area of relief by 12th Div. T.M. Batteries.	
ROZIERE	6-7		Nothing to report.	
HARDINVAL	8		Moved to HARDINVAL.	
BOURDON	9		Moved to BOURDON.	
"	10-17		Nothing to report.	
ST.SAUVEUR	18		Moved to ST.SAUVEUR.	
AUBIGNY	19		Moved to AUBIGNY.	
HANGARD	20		Moved to HANGARD.	
IGNAUCOURT	21		Moved to IGNAUCOURT.	
"	22-27		Nothing to report.	
ROSIERES	28		Moved to ROSIERES, leaving rear parties at IGNAUCOURT.	

Ammn. expenditure for month - 111 rounds.

Maggoot 2/Lt
for Commanding Z/35 T.M. Battery.

SECRET.

War Diary

of

V/35 Trench Mortar Battery

From 1st March to 31st March 1917.

Vol. 4.

H.E. Waller   Commanding V/35 Trench Mortar Battery

WAR DIARY
or
INTELLIGENCE SUMMARY

(Erase heading not required.)

Army Form C. 2118.

Instructions regarding War Diaries and Intelligence Summaries are contained in F. S. Regs., Part II. and the Staff Manual respectively. Title Pages will be prepared in manuscript.

Place	Date	Hour	Summary of Events and Information	Remarks and references to Appendices
GNAUCOURT	1.3.19 to 8.3.19		Battery employed in lurking parties at its waggon lines & to 15 y - 190 Bdes R.F.A. MED.	
GNAUCOURT	9.3.19		All lurking parties cealed Proceed at IGNAUCOURT	
ROSIERES	16.3.19		Battery marched to - Billeted at ROSIERES MED.	
"	11.3.19 to 14.3.19		Battery employed in carrying party at night carrying material for construction of 2" T.M. emplacements MED.	
"	15.3.19 16.3.19 16.3.19		Employed carrying 2 T.M. ammunition to emplacements at night. MED. Rtn H.M. MICHIE, R.F.A. struck off strength to England for duty D.A.R.O. 615 MED.	
MAUCOURT	17.3.19		Roadmaking bridging trenches evacuated by enemy Abroite CHILLY. Marched to MAUCOURT. Billeted in dugouts MED.	
	18.3.19		Nothing to report MED.	
	19.3.19		Employed in collecting hire in divisional area MED.	
	20.3.19 to 25.3.19		Work continued MED.	
WARVILLERS	25.3.19		Battery marched to billeted L WARVILLERS MED.	

WAR DIARY or INTELLIGENCE SUMMARY

Army Form C. 2118.

Place	Date	Hour	Summary of Events and Information	Remarks and references to Appendices
MESNIL-ST-NICAISE	26.3.19		Battery proceeded to billets at MESNIL-ST-NICAISE by motor lorry. #2w.	
"	27.3.19		Employed in forming IV Corps Ammunition Dump. #2w.	
"	28.3.19 to 31.3.19		Employed in mending roads, Handing Off loading ammunition at Dump. #2w.	
			Ammunition expenditure for the month — NIL #2w	

H. Thraller
Major R.G.A.
Comdg V/35 Battery

SECRET

War Diary

of

X/35. Trench Mortar Battery

From 1st March to 31st March 1917

Vol. 9

A Leckie 2nd Lt
RFA
Commanding X/35 Trench Mortar
Battery

WAR DIARY or INTELLIGENCE SUMMARY

Army Form C. 2118.

X 35 T M BATTERY

Place	Date	Hour	Summary of Events and Information	Remarks and references to Appendices
	MAR. 1 to 7		Battery in Rest Billets at IGNAUCOURT. Nothing to report.	OK
	8		Moved to ROSIERES.	OK
	9		Nothing to report	OK
	10		Nothing to report	OK
	11		Moved to MAUCOURT	OK
	12 to 16		Work on preparation of gun positions. Carrying material and mortars to battery position.	OK
	17		In action S.E. of CHILLY. Battery opened fire on enemy wire at 7 a.m. as per bombardment programme. Mortar position struck by 10.5 c.m. H.E. shell at 7.25 a.m. 2 men killed and two wounded. Battery ceased fire at 12 a.m.	OK
	18		Nothing to report	OK
	19 to 23		2ND LT. P.M. LECKIE struck off strength wounded. Battery relaying telephone wire in Divisional area.	OK and PM Leckie 2nd TMB X 35 TMB OC 11 A/4/11
	24		Moved to WARVILLERS	OK
	25		Moved to MESNIL ST NICAISE	OK
	26			
	27 to 31		Battery employed with working party on Corps Ammunition Dump, MESNIL.	OK

SECRET

Vol 9

War Diary

of

Y/35 Trench Mortar Battery

From 1st Mar to 31st March 1917

Vol. 9

J. G. Whitehead. Lieut
for Commanding Y/35 Trench Mortar Battery

WAR DIARY
or
INTELLIGENCE SUMMARY.

Army Form C. 2118.

Place	Date	Hour	Summary of Events and Information	Remarks and references to Appendices
EGNAUCOURT.	March 1917. 1st	—	Battery resting	Yes
	2nd	—	Battery moved into new trench area & billets at ROSIERES.	Yes
ROSIERES	3-3	—	Battery resting.	Yes
	4.12	—	Nothing to report.	Yes
	5.12	—	Nothing to report.	Yes
	6.12	—	Nothing to report.	Yes
	7.12	—	Nothing to report.	Yes
	8.12	—	Nothing to report.	Yes
	9.12	—	Nothing to report.	Yes
	10.12	—	Nothing to report.	Yes
	11.12	—	Nothing to report.	Yes
	12.12	—	Position selected and commenced. Lieut. J. G. WHITEHEAD reports for duty attached from 17th L.F.	Yes
	13.12	—	Work continued.	Yes
	14.12	—	Work continued.	Yes
	15.12	—	Battery proceeded to billets at MAUCOURT, men employed in carrying up ammunition.	Yes
MAUCOURT.	16.12	—	To gun positions at night. Main ammunition taken up. Battery has 150 men of Infantry & 50 D.A.C. to assist. The enemy unusually quiet.	Yes

Army Form C. 2118.

WAR DIARY
or
INTELLIGENCE SUMMARY.
(Erase heading not required.)

Place	Date	Hour	Summary of Events and Information	Remarks and references to Appendices
CHILLY.	March 1917 17th	6.30 a.m. 1.0 a.m. 4.0 p.m.	Motors reported an enemy wire. Bombardment commenced on enemy line by artillery. Motors fires no time. Firing continues to prosecution. Firing are the orders to cease. Infantry are seen to be taken. No man lands in matte platoon, on the night W. Bombards & Lydd Whitters + 6 men reliefs one to enemy's line.	
	8.0		Pons J. unoccupied by the enemy. Battery settles to Maucourt. British Infantry continues to advance during the night.	
			During firing one water under Cpl. McLaughlan has a premature. The emplacement been destroyed & the Gofriel wounded in the head. Ammunition expended during the day 150 rounds.	
MAUCOURT.	18th.	—	Battery clears emplacement. 2 hours J. had notice to start.	do.
	19th.	—	No. 11tn. 16 up.	do.
	20th.	—	Battery emplaces in collection one on Downward Road.	do.
	21st.		Work continued.	do.
	22nd.		do.	do.
	23rd.		do. continued.	do.

Army Form C. 2118.

WAR DIARY
or
INTELLIGENCE SUMMARY.
(Erase heading not required.)

Instructions regarding War Diaries and Intelligence Summaries are contained in F. S. Regs., Part II. and the Staff Manual respectively. Title pages will be prepared in manuscript.

Place	Date	Hour	Summary of Events and Information	Remarks and references to Appendices
MAUCOURT.	March 1917 24th	-	Nil. continued.	
	25th.	-	Battery proceeded to WARVILLERS.	
WARVILLERS	26th.	-	Battery proceeded to MESNIL-ST-NICAISE.	
MESNIL-ST-NICAISE	27th.	-	Battery employed on forming an Ammunition Dump.	
	28th.	-	Battery employed loading & unloading.	
	29th.	-	Battery continue on work.	
	30th.	-	Battery continue on work.	
	31st.	-	Battery continue on work.	

J.C. Watters Lt
A.Y/35 Battery

SECRET

War Diary

of.

Z/38 Trench Mortar Battery

From 1st March to 31st March 1917

Vol. 9

J. Taggart 2/Lt
for Commanding Z/38 Trench Mortar Battery

Z/35 Trench Mortar Battery
March 1917

WAR DIARY
or
~~INTELLIGENCE SUMMARY~~

Army Form C. 2118.

(Erase heading not required.)

Instructions regarding War Diaries and Intelligence Summaries are contained in F. S. Regs., Part II. and the Staff Manual respectively. Title pages will be prepared in manuscript.

Place	Date	Hour	Summary of Events and Information	Remarks and references to Appendices
	March 1917			
IGNAUCOURT	1st		Battery moved from IGNAUCOURT to ROSIÈRES	gps
ROSIÈRES	2nd to 11th		Nothing to report.	gps
ROSIÈRES	12th to 17th		Working parties, digging gunpits, and carrying parties. One gunner wounded on 16th.	gps
ROSIÈRES	18th		Battery moved from ROSIÈRES to MAUCOURT	gps
MAUCOURT	19th to 25th		Were collecting on Devisemed area.	gps
MAUCOURT	25th		Battery moved from MAUCOURT to WARVILLERS	gps
WARVILLERS	26th to 27th		Nothing to report	gps
WARVILLERS	28th		Battery moved from WARVILLERS to 4th ARMY School of Mortars	gps
4th ARMY School of Mortars	29th to 31st		Nothing to report	gps

Huggett 2/Lt R.F.A.
for o/c Z/35 T.M.B.
4/4/17

SECRET

Vol I

War Diary

of

V/35 Trench Mortar Battery

1st April 1917 to 30th April 1917

Volume 8

H. Waller Capt. R.F.A.
Commanding V/35 Trench Mortar Battery.

Army Form C. 2118.

WAR DIARY
or
INTELLIGENCE SUMMARY
(Erase heading not required.)

1/3 S. Trench mortar bty

April 1919

Place	Date	Hour	Summary of Events and Information	Remarks and references to Appendices
MESNIL-ST NICAISE	Apl 1-14		Battery employed as working party loading and unloading ammunition at 10 corps Dumps and Railhead. MEV.	
MONCHY-LAGACHE	15		Battery moved to MONCHY-LAGACHE. MEV.	
"	16		Battery employed as working party on Divisional Ammun Dumps. MEV.	
	20			
	21			
	17		CAPT W.H. PRICE (NOTTS & DERBY REGT) struck off strength prior to transper to R.G.A. MEV.	
	22		Battery employed repairing road near POEUILLY. MEV.	
	20			
	25			
VERMAND	26		Moved to VERMAND. MEV.	
	27		2. LT F.J. PREWITT joined from 159 Bde R.F.A. MEV.	
	27			
"	6		Battery employed in filling in mine crater in road at VERMAND. MEV.	
	30			

V.E.Allen Capt R. F.a.
O. comdg 1/3 S. Trench mortar bty.

SECRET

War Diary

of

X/35 Trench Mortar Battery

From 1st April 1917   To 30th April 1917

Volume 10

C.M. Leckie 2nd Lieut R.F.A.
Commanding X/35. Trench Mortar Battery

Army Form C. 2118.

X/35. Trench Mortar Battery

WAR DIARY
or
INTELLIGENCE SUMMARY.
(Erase heading not required.)

April 1917.

Instructions regarding War Diaries and Intelligence Summaries are contained in F. S. Regs., Part II. and the Staff Manual respectively. Title pages will be prepared in manuscript.

Place	Date	Hour	Summary of Events and Information	Remarks and references to Appendices
MESNIL ST NICAISE	1 to 1st		Battery employed as working party loading and off-loading ammunition at 10 army's 10 cents and Railhead	O.K.R
MONCHY LAGACHE	3		2nd Lt P. McLECKIE rejoins from hospital and is posted to Battery	O.K.R
	15		Battery moved to MONCHY-LAGACHE.	O.K.R
"	16 to 21		Battery employed as working party on Divisional Ammunition Dump	O.K.R
"	22 to 23		Battery employed repairing road at POEUILLY.	O.K.R
VERMAND	26		Battery moved to VERMAND	O.K.R
"	26 to 30		Battery employed filling in mine craters in road at VERMAND.	O.K.R

O.K.Leckie
Lieut. R.F.A.
Commanding X/35 Trench Mortar Battery

SECRET

War Diary

of

Y/35 Trench Mortar Battery

From 1st April 1917   To 30th April 1917

Volume 10

(James P. Whitford)
Lieut:
Y/35 Trench Mortar Battery

SECRET

Y/35 Trench Mortar Battery

Army Form C. 2118.

WAR DIARY
or
INTELLIGENCE SUMMARY
(Erase heading not required.)

April 1917.

Place	Date	Hour	Summary of Events and Information	Remarks and references to Appendices
MESNIL ST NICAISE	1st to 8.		Battery employed as working party, loading and off loading ammunition at dumps and Railhead.	
"	8.		LT. T.G. WHITEHEAD posted to battery from 17th LANCS. FUSILIERS.	
"	9.		LT. C.W. PULFORD and 4 O.R. rejoin after refresher course at IV Army School of mortars.	
"	9th to 13th.		Work on Ammunition Dumps continued.	
"	14th.		Practice shoot carried out on old enemy trench, 10 rds fired.	
MONCHY LAGACHE	15th		Battery moved to MONCHY-LAGACHE.	
"	16th to 21st.		Battery employed as working party on Divisional Ammunition Dumps.	
"	22nd to 25th.		Battery employed in repairing roads near POEUILLY.	
"	26th		Battery moved to VERMAND.	
VERMAND	26th to 30th.		Battery employed in filling in mine craters in roads at VERMAND.	

Ja. G. White. Capt.
Y/35. Trench Mortar Battery.

SECRET

War Diary

of

Z/35 Trench Mortar Battery

From 1st April 1917   To 30th April 1917

Volume 10

R.H. Spalding. Lieut
Commanding Z/35 Trench Mortar Battery

Army Form C. 2118.

Z/35 Trench Mortar Battery

WAR DIARY
or
INTELLIGENCE SUMMARY.
(Erase heading not required.)

April 1917

Place	Date	Hour	Summary of Events and Information	Remarks and references to Appendices
VAUX-EN-AMIENOIS	April 7th & 8th		Battery marching at IV Army School of Mortars. Received excellent report from Commandant of School.	App XXI Mortars-PS → App x 1
MESNIL-ST-NICAISSE	9th		Moved by lorries to MESNIL-ST-NICAISSE.	RBF
"	10th & 12th		Battery employed in constructing pillars.	RBF
"	13th		Constructed a 90° traverse T.M bed in old enemy line near MESNIL-ST-NICAISSE.	RBF
"	14th		Tested bed by firing 10 rounds good results.	RBF
MONCHY-LAGACHE	15th		Moved to MONCHY-LAGACHE	RBF
"	16th & 20th		Battery employed at Divisional Ammunition Dumps	RBF
"	21st			
"	22nd & 23rd		Battery employed in repairing roads near POEUILLY	RBF
VERMAND	25th		Moved to VERMAND	RBF
"	26th & 30th		Battery employed in filling in mine crater in road at VERMAND.	RBF

Ronald J. [signature] Lieut

"P" *War Diary Appendix 1.*

IV CORPS.

REPORT ON Z/35 TRENCH MORTAR BATTERY.

STRENGTH.	Officers	N.C.O's	O.R's	TOTAL.
	2	5	18	25

Officers.

Lieut: R.F. SPALDING - A capable B.C. Energetic and keen.

Knowledge of Gun & Equipment	- Very Good.
Drill.	- Very Good.
Delivery.	- Good.
Interior Economy.	- Very Good.
Tactical.	- Very Good.

N.C.Os & Men.

PHYSIQUE	- Very Good.
Drill & knowledge of Gun.	- Very Good.
Discipline.	- Very Good.
Interior Economy	- Good.
Equipment.	- Very Good.

Sd. E.W. PLUMER.
Lt.Colonel, R.A.
Commandant School of Mortars, Fourth Army.

SCHOOL OF MORTARS, FOURTH ARMY.

REPORT ON DEFICIENCIES ON GUNS BROUGHT TO SCHOOL BY :-

Z/35 T. M. Battery, 35th Division, IVth Corps.

Medium Mortars.

Gun No.	DEFICIENCIES.
1140.	Complete.
95.	Complete.
743.	Complete.
170.	Complete.

SECRET

Vol XI

War Diary

of

V/35. Trench Mortar Battery

From 1st May 1917   To 31st May 1917

(Volume 9)

E.W.R. Fitzgerald, Capt.
D.T.M.O. 35th Division
for
O.C. V/35 Trench Mortar Battery

Army Form C. 2118.

WAR DIARY
or
INTELLIGENCE SUMMARY.
(Erase heading not required.)

V/35 Trench Mortar Battery

May 1917

Instructions regarding War Diaries and Intelligence Summaries are contained in F. S. Regs., Part II. and the Staff Manual respectively. Title pages will be prepared in manuscript.

Place	Date	Hour	Summary of Events and Information	Remarks and references to Appendices
VERMAND	1st to 21st		Battery employed in maintaining road at VERMAND	Enr. I
MONCHY-LAGACHE	22nd		Battery moved to MONCHY-LAGACHE	Enr. I
DOINGT	23rd to 24th		Battery moved to DOINGT. At DOINGT.	Enr. I, 9 or R.9
VAUX-EN-AMIENOIS	25th		Battery proceeded to Yourch Arm School of Mortars	Enr. I
— " —	26th to 30th		Battery remodelling at School of Mortars	Enr. I
— " —	31st			

E.W.R. Wybergh
2/Lt M.O. 35th Div.
for V/35 Trench Mortar Battery

"SECRET"

War Diary

of

X/35 Trench Mortar Battery

From 1st May 1917   To 31st May 1917

(Volume II)

C. W. Backwell, Lieut.
X/35 Trench Mortar Battery

Army Form C. 2118.

X/35 Trench Mortar Battery

WAR DIARY
or
INTELLIGENCE SUMMARY.
(Erase heading not required.)

May 1917

Instructions regarding War Diaries and Intelligence Summaries are contained in F. S. Regs., Part II. and the Staff Manual respectively. Title pages will be prepared in manuscript.

Place	Date	Hour	Summary of Events and Information	Remarks and references to Appendices
VERMAND	1st to 21st		Battery employed in maintaining road at VERMAND	(a)X
MONCHY-LAGACHE	22nd		Battery moved to MONCHY-LAGACHE	(b)X
PERONNE	23rd		Battery moved to PERONNE	(c)X
D.9 central 26 6/d sh 62c			Battery moved to D.9 central sheet 62c. 14 Divn rail attached to 159th Brigade R.F.A. as working parties	(d)X
"	" to 31st		Remainder of personnel employed as working parties on Divisional Ammunition Dump	(e)X
"	31st		2.L. C.W. BACKWELL 20TH LANCS. FUSILIERS proceeded on 10 days leave 28.5.17 (away 28. to 10.6.17) 30.5.17. and 26.5.17	(f)X

C.W.Backwell 2/Lt
for O.C. X/35 Trench Mortar Battery

SECRET

War Diary

of

Y/35 Trench Mortar Battery

From 1st May 1917 To 31st May 1917

(Volume 11)

Jas. G. Whitehead Lieut
Y/35 Trench Mortar Battery

Army Form C. 2118.

Y/35 Trench mortar battery

WAR DIARY
or
INTELLIGENCE SUMMARY
(Erase heading not required.)

May 1917

Place	Date	Hour	Summary of Events and Information	Remarks and references to Appendices
VERMAND	1 to 10th		Battery employed in repairing road at VERMAND	
VAUX-EN-AMIENOIS	11th		Battery proceeded to IV Army School of mortars at VAUX-EN-AMIENOIS.	
"	12th to 24th		Battery redrilling at school of mortars	
PERONNE	25th		Battery proceeded to Reinforcements Camp. PERONNE	
"	26th		Nothing to report.	
D.9 central Sheet 62.c.	27th		Battery proceeded to D.9 central (Sheet 62.c.)	
"	28th to 31st		Battery employed as working party on Divl Ammunition Dump.	

J.G. Botteas. Lieut
Y/35 Trench mortar battery

SECRET

War Diary

of

Z/35 Trench Mortar Battery

From 1st May 1917.   To 31st May 1917.

(Volume 11)

J.W. Taggart   Lieut. R.F.A.
Z/35 Trench Mortar Battery

Army Form C. 2118.

Z/55 Trench Mortar Battery

WAR DIARY
or
INTELLIGENCE SUMMARY

(Erase heading not required.)

Mar 1919

Instructions regarding War Diaries and Intelligence Summaries are contained in F. S. Regs., Part II. and the Staff Manual respectively. Title Pages will be prepared in manuscript.

Place	Date	Hour	Summary of Events and Information	Remarks and references to Appendices
VERMAND	1/3 to 21/3		Battery employed maintaining road at VERMAND	
MONCHY-LAGACHE	22 Mar		Battery march to MONCHY-LAGACHE	
PERONNE	28 Mar		Battery moved to PERONNE	
D.G. Central and Spare exc	29 Mar		Battery moved to D.G. Central (short 2.5e), and remainder attached to 159th Bde R.F.A. on wrecking trains.	
	25/3 to 31/3		Work under the 159 Bde R.F.A. continued.	

J.F. Taggart Lieut. R.F.A.
for O.C. Z/55 Trench Mortar Battery

SECRET.

War Diary

of

V/35 Trench Mortar Battery

From 1st June 1917   To 30th June 1917

Volume 10

E.W.R. Fitzgerald. Capt.
for. O.C. V/35 Trench Mortar Battery

1/35 Trench Mortar Battery   Army Form C. 2118.

WAR DIARY
or
INTELLIGENCE SUMMARY.
(Erase heading not required.)

June 1917

Place	Date	Hour	Summary of Events and Information	Remarks and references to Appendices
VAUX-EN-AMIENOIS	1 to 5		Battery reassembling at IV Army School of Mortars.	Exet 7.
QUINCONCE	6th		Battery moved to QUINCONCE Reinforcement Camp	Exet 7.
D.9 Central y.d. Sheet 62c	7th		Battery moved to D.9 Central (Sheet 62c)	Exet 7.
"	8th		Nothing to report.	Exet 7.
"	9th		46 Other Ranks attached to 35th Div Arty. Working Parties (Headquarters X.13.a.5d.3/4.5E)	Exet 7.
"	10th to 30th		Work under 35th Div Arty. Working Parties continued. Remainder of battery at T.M. Headquarters D.9 Central.	Exet 7.

E.W.R. Shy Cartwright
for Major R.F.A.
Commanding 1/35 Trench Mortar Battery

SECRET

War Diary

of

X/35 Trench Mortar Battery

From 1st June 1917 To 30th June 1917

Volume 12

CHLeckie   Lieut R.F.A.
Commanding X/35 Trench Mortar Battery

Army Form C. 2118.

WAR DIARY
or
INTELLIGENCE SUMMARY.   X 35 T.M. BATTERY.
(*Erase heading not required.*)

Instructions regarding War Diaries and Intelligence Summaries are contained in F. S. Regs., Part II. and the Staff Manual respectively. Title pages will be prepared in manuscript.

Place	Date	Hour	Summary of Events and Information	Remarks and references to Appendices
NURLU	1 to 7		Attached as working party to 159th BDE. R.F.A.	O.K
VAUX-EN-AMIENNOIS	8		Travelling to VAUX-EN-AMIENNOIS	O.K
	9 to 18		On Course of Instruction at 4th ARMY. SCHOOL OF MORTARS	O.K
do.			"	
PERONNE	19		Travelling to PERONNE. Billets in REST CAMP.	O.K
RONSSOY	20		Travelling to RONSSOY.	O.K
do.	21		In action at GILLEMONT FARM. Building mortar positions at night. 2nd LT. C.W. BACKWELL and 2.O.R. killed and 1.O.R. wounded during enemy raid on farm.	O.K
do.	22 to 30		In action at GILLEMONT FARM.	O.K
do.			do.	O.K

R.W. Yuckie Lt
O.C. / X 35 T.M.B
1-7-17

SECRET

War Diary

of

V/35 Trench Mortar Battery

From 1st June 1917   To 30th June 1917

Volume 12

E.W.R. FitzGerald
Capt
for O.C. V/35 Trench Mortar Battery

V/35 Trench Mortar Battery   June 1917   Army Form C. 2118.

WAR DIARY
or
INTELLIGENCE SUMMARY.
(Erase heading not required.)

Place	Date	Hour	Summary of Events and Information	Remarks and references to Appendices
D.9 central Sh 36.N.W.c.6.8.d.	1st		Battery employed as working party on Civil Ammunition Dump	Ap Z.
N.13.a Sheet 36c.S.E.	9th	9 am	Battery moved to N.13.a Sheet 36c.S.E. on attaches to 55th Div Arty working party.	App. Z.
—	10th to 30th		Work on gun positions under O.C. 55th Div Arty. Working party continued.	App. Z.

Eric Styles, Capt.
for Commanding V/35 Trench Mortar Battery.

SECRET

War Diary

of

Z/35 Trench Mortar Battery

From 1st June 1917   To 30th June 1917

Volume 12

J.H. Taggart, Lieut R.F.A.
Commanding Z/35 Trench Mortar By.

Army Form C. 2118.

WAR DIARY
or
INTELLIGENCE SUMMARY.
(Erase heading not required.)

Instructions regarding War Diaries and Intelligence Summaries are contained in F.S. Regs., Part II. and the Staff Manual respectively. Title pages will be prepared in manuscript.

Place	Date	Hour	Summary of Events and Information	Remarks and references to Appendices
	JUNE 1917			
NURLU	1 to 27		Attached to 159 Bde. as working parties	9th
NURLU	27 28		Attached to 35 D.A. as working parties	9th
NURLU	29		Moved from NURLU to RONSSOY	9th
RONSSOY	30		Preparing gun positions behind GILLEMONT FARM	9th

JMHaggart 2Lt. R.F.A.
O/c Z/35 T.M.B.

SECRET

War Diary

of

V/35 Trench Mortar Battery

From 1st July 1917   To 31st July 1917

(Volume 11)

H.E. Waller   Capt. R.F.A.
Commanding V/35 Trench Mortar Battery

Army Form C. 2118.

1/35 Trench Mortar Battery   July 1917

WAR DIARY
or
INTELLIGENCE SUMMARY.
(Erase heading not required.)

Instructions regarding War Diaries and Intelligence Summaries are contained in F. S. Regs., Part II. and the Staff Manual respectively. Title pages will be prepared in manuscript.

Place	Date	Hour	Summary of Events and Information	Remarks and references to Appendices
D.9 central Sheet 62c	1st		40 Other Ranks attached to 35th Div Arty Working Party reform Trench mortar to dgrs at D.9 central (Sheet 62c.) MRs	
E.18.c.80.50 Sht 62c	2nd		Battery moved to E.18.c.80.50 (Sheet 62c.) (Nearly near ST EMILIE). 18 Other Ranks attached as working party to 164grs 35 Div Div Arty MRs	
"	3rd		Working to reform MRs	
"	4th		Remainder of Battery moved to DRIENCOURT MRs	
DRIENCOURT	5th		Commenced Work Traymaking under O.C. 35 Div Train MRs	
"	6th		"	
"	7th		Traymaking and work as to dgrs 35 Div Div Arty continued MRs	
"	8th		2 Lt R.M. LECKIE R.F.A. posted from 1/35 Trench Mortar Battery MRs	
"	9th & 10th		Traymaking and work as to dgrs 35 Div Arty continued MRs	
"	11th		2 Lt F.J. PREWITT R.F.A. admitted to Hospital and evacuated to 34 S.o.S MRs	
E.18.c.80.50 Sheet 62c.	12th		Battery, with exception of 8 other ranks remaining Traymaking reform Trench Mortar to dgrs at E.18.c.80.50. MRs	
"	13th		Work on 20 emy Trench Mortar Positions at F.11.b.50.35. and F.18.a.10.10 commenced MRs	
"	14th 15th		Work continued MRs	
"	16th		2 Lt D.H. URQUHART R.F.A. joins from base. Work continued MRs	
"	17th to 27th		On 9.45" Trench Mortars taken on charge. Work on positions continued MRs	

WAR DIARY
or
INTELLIGENCE SUMMARY.

Army Form C. 2118.

Place	Date	Hour	Summary of Events and Information	Remarks and references to Appendices
E.18.c.60.50 Sh 62 c.a.	28		Fired 6 rounds registering enemy trench at A.13.d.30.60. by aeroplane. T.M.s. Lt. D. HURQUHART proceeded to 3rd Army School of mortars for course in Heavy mortars. T.M.s.	
"	29th to 31st		Work on positions continued. T.M.s.	
			Ammunition expenditure for the month = 6 rounds. T.M.s.	

H. Butler Capt. R.F.A.
Commanding V/52 Trench Mortar Battery.

SECRET

War Diary

of

X/35 Trench Mortar Battery

From 1st July 1917   To 31st July 17

(Volume 13)

James G. Whitehead.
Lieut.
Commanding X/35 Trench Mortar Battery

WAR DIARY or INTELLIGENCE SUMMARY.

Army Form C. 2118.

X/35. Trench Mortar Battery.   July 1917

(Erase heading not required.)

Instructions regarding War Diaries and Intelligence Summaries are contained in F.S. Regs., Part II. and the Staff Manual respectively. Title pages will be prepared in manuscript.

Place	Date	Hour	Summary of Events and Information	Remarks and references to Appendices
RONSSOY	1st		Reconnoitred emplacements near GUILLEMONT FARM. Took up guns and amn. dump to position.	
"	2nd		Carried up ammunition, and fired no. 3A front of naw position. Experimental 32 rounds on GUILLEMONT FARM.	
"	3rd			
"	4th		Guns brought down to park in ST EMILIE.	
ST EMILIE	5th		Returned to billets in quarry.	
"	6th		Nothing to report.	
"	6.9.0.		A/Lt. P.M. LEGRIE posted to X/35 trench mortar battery.	
"	8th		Lt. T.G. WHITEHEAD posted to X/35 trench mortar battery from Y/35 T.M.B.	
"	9th		At BARRACLOUGH HOUSE.	
"	10th 6.15 W		Nothing to report.	
"	11th		Work on previous opposite GUILLEMONT FARM commenced.	
"	12th			
"	"		Work on previous continued.	
"	31st		Ammunition inspection from the road - 15 rounds.	

M. W. Ellis. Lieut
Commanding X/35 Trench Mortar Bty.

SECRET

War Diary

of

1/35 Trench Mortar Battery

From 1st July 17   To 31st July 17

(Volume 13)

C.W. Pulford Lieut R.F.A.
Commanding 1/35 Trench Mortar Battery

Army Form C. 2118.

WAR DIARY
or
INTELLIGENCE SUMMARY

1/35 Trench Mortar Battery   July 17

(Erase heading not required.)

Instructions regarding War Diaries and Intelligence Summaries are contained in F. S. Regs., Part II. and the Staff Manual respectively. Title pages will be prepared in manuscript.

Place	Date	Hour	Summary of Events and Information	Remarks and references to Appendices
D.9 central sheet 62c	1st		Battery ceased work under 38th Div Arty. Moving from present Trench Mortar positions to dugouts at D.9 central (Sheet 62c)	
E.18.c.60.50 sheet 62c	2nd		Battery moved to E.18.c.60.50 (Quarry near ST. EMILIE)	
"	3rd to 8th		Nothing to report.	
"	9th		Lt. J.G. WHITEHEAD posted to 1/35 Trench Mortar Battery	
"	10th to 13th		Nothing to report.	
"	14th		Work on Trench Mortar Battery positions in F.18.c. commenced	
"	15th to 31st		Work on positions continued	

E.B. Scott (Lt)   Lieut. R.F.A.
Commanding 1/35 Trench Mortar Bty.

SECRET

War Diary

of

Z/35 Trench Mortar Battery

From 1st July 17   To 31st July 17

(Volume 13)

J. Daggnub
Lieut R.F.A.
Commanding Z/35 Trench Mortar Bty

Z/35 Trench Mortar Battery   July 1917

WAR DIARY
or
INTELLIGENCE SUMMARY.
(Erase heading not required.)

Army Form C. 2118.

Instructions regarding War Diaries and Intelligence Summaries are contained in F.S. Regs., Part II. and the Staff Manual respectively. Title pages will be prepared in manuscript.

Place	Date	Hour	Summary of Events and Information	Remarks and references to Appendices
RONSSOY	July 1, 2		Lt. R.F. Shielding, struck off the strength with effect from 25/5/17.	AW
"	3		Work and TM Emplacements at F.18.c. (State o.c.)	AW
"	4		Ammunition expended 54 rounds	AW
"	5		Moved from RONSSOY to T.M. H.Q. at E.18.c.30.50.	AW
St. Emilie	6 & 7		Nothing to report.	AW
"	8		2Lt. J.D. TAGGART posted to command Z/35 T.M.B. with acting rank of lieutenant from 26.5.17.	AW
"	9 & 11		Nothing to report	AW
"	12		2Lt. W.S. CAUVIN joins from 19 D.L.I	AW
"	13		Nothing to report.	AW
"	14 & 31		Work on positions in F.18.C. (State o.c.)	AW

JD Taggart 2/Lt RIF
O/C Z/35 T.M.B.

SECRET

Vol 14

War Diary

of

V/35 Trench Mortar Battery

From 1st Aug 17   To 31st Aug 17

Volume 12.

CM Leckie Lieut R.F.A.
for Officer Commanding V/35 Trench Mortar Bty

V/35 Trench Mortar Battery

WAR DIARY or INTELLIGENCE SUMMARY.

(Erase heading not required.)

Place	Date	Hour	Summary of Events and Information	Remarks and references to Appendices
E.18.c.80.50 S.d.c.60.12.d.	1.5		Work on emplacements continued.	OiC
"	15th		One 9.45" Lang French mortar mark II taken in charge.	OiC
"	15th		Work on emplacements continued.	OiC
"	15th		2Lt D.H URQUHART reports from course at III Army School of mortars. Supervision on emplacements continued.	OiC BiC OiC
"	16th		Mortars mounted in emplacements.	
"	17th		2Lt D.H URQUHART admitted to hospital sick.	
"	18th		Bombardment, much hostile machine gun and trench mortar activity on the KNOLL and near GILLEMONT FARM carried out. Expenditure 34 rds.	OiC
"	19th		Bombarded trenches, etc., in support of action on the KNOLL and at GILLEMONT FARM. Expenditure 25 rds.	OiC
"	20th		12 rounds fired in reply to S.O.S. KNOLL and GILLEMONT, and in answer to S.O.S. KNOL- and GILLEMONT. Also in French trench mortars. Expenditure 32 rounds.	OiC OiC
"	21.		Nothing to report.	OiC
"	22.&} 23rd}			OiC
"	24th		Fire used in retaliation to enemy trench mortar fire and in reply to S.O.S. during enemy attack on our trenches at GILLEMONT FARM in the morning and in support of our counter attack on 4.30 p.m. Expenditure 30 rounds.	OiC
	25th			OiC

SECRET

War Diary

of

X/35 Trench Mortar Battery

From 1st Aug 17   To 31st Aug 17

Volume 14

Barraclough 2/Lt
/o/c X/35 Trench Mortar Battery

INTELLIGENCE SUMMARY.

(Erase heading not required.)

Place	Date	Hour	Summary of Events and Information	Remarks and references to Appendices
E.18.c.60.60	29/3/17		Battery in action at: F.11.B.30.4.t and F.18.c.10.30. Expended 29 rounds.	O.K.
			Total expenditure for the month 168 rounds. Own called.	O.K.

Appendix O.V. to M2 TMB

SECRET

War Diary

of

X/35 Trench Mortar Battery

From 1st Aug 17   To 31st Aug 17

Volume 14.

Darraclough. 2Lt.
for O/C X/35 Trench Mortar Battery

X 35 Trench Mortar Battery.

WAR DIARY or **INTELLIGENCE SUMMARY.**

Army Form C. 2118.

August 1917.

Place	Date	Hour	Summary of Events and Information	Remarks and references to Appendices
E.18.c.80.30 Sheet 62c	1–14	–	Bty. employed shelling positions in F.18 a & c.	SB
	15th	–	2nd Lt. S. BARRACLOUGH R.F.A. returned from course at 3rd Army Sch. of Mortars.	SB
	16–19th	–	Bty. carrying Amm.	SB
	20th	–	Bty. relieved Y & Z Btys. in the Line at GILLEMONT FARM. Fired on enemy trenches in reply to S.O.S. Expended 25 rnds.	SB
	21st	–	Fired on enemy trench in reply to S.O.S. Expended 23 rnds.	SB
	22–24th	–	Amm. expended 32 rnds.	SB
	25th	–	Hostile counter attack on GILLEMONT FARM. Fired 20 rnds. during enemy attack.	SB
	26th	–	Bty. relieved by Y. & Z. Btys.	SB
	27th	–	Nothing to report.	SB
	28–31st	–	Bty. in action. Fired 55 rnds.	SB

TOTAL EXPENDITURE for month 175 rounds
CASUALTIES — NIL.

S. Barraclough 2nd Lt. R.F.A.
O.C. X.35 T.M.B.

SECRET

War Diary

of

Y/35 Trench Mortar Battery

From 1st Aug 17   To 31st Aug 17

Volume 14.

C W Rilford, Lieut R.F.A.
Commanding Y/35 Trench Mortar Battery

WAR DIARY or INTELLIGENCE SUMMARY.

(Erase heading not required.)

Y/35 Trench Mortar Battery   Army Form

Place	Date 1917	Hour	Summary of Events and Information	Remarks and references to Appendices
Shut 62c E 19 C 80 50	Aug 16/15		Work on Battery positions F 18 A 50 00.	6x5P
	16/17		Guns (four) put in position at F 18 A 50 00.	6x5P
	18		Bombarded hostile trenches and cut wire for attack on enemy trenches around GILLEMONT. FARM. Amm⁰ Expenditure 200 rounds. Casualties Nil.	6x5P
	19		Infantry attacked and captured enemy trenches east of GILLEMONT FARM. Amm⁰ Expend. 550 rounds.	6x5P
	20		Fired in reply to S.O.S. GILLEMONT by X/35 T.M.B. Battery relieved.	6x5P
	21/24		Battery on Ammunition carrying.	6x5P
	25		Bombarded enemy trenches around GILLEMONT in support of Inf Counter attack. Amm⁰ Expend. 413 rounds.	6x5P
	26/31		Battery in action at F 18 A 50 00. Amm⁰ Expend a 335 rds. Casualties Nil.	6x5T
			Total Amm⁰ Expend. for month 335 rds.	

6x3 Pulsford Lt RFA
O/c Y/35. T.M.B.

SECRET

War Diary

of

Z/35 Trench Mortar Battery

From 1st Aug 17   To 31st Aug 17

Volume 14

J. Taggart   Lieut R.F.A.
Commanding Z/35 Trench Mortar Battery

WAR DIARY

Z/35 Trench Mortar Battery
August 1917
Army Form C. 2118.

Place	Date	Hour	Summary of Events and Information	Remarks and references to Appendices
S+ EMILE	August 12th 13th		Preparing battery positions at GUILLEMONT FARM. Ammunition carrying up.	
	16th 17th		Guns moved into action. Positions prepared for action.	
	18th		Wire cutting infantry GUILLEMONT FARM. 250 rds fired	
	19th		Support of attack on G'x'LLEMONT FARM. 25 rds fired. Battery relieved by X/145	
	20 21		Preparing new positions. Ammunition carrying. Battery relieved X/145.	
	22		Enemy counter-attack. 22 rds fired	
	23		Battery relieved by X/145	
	24		Work on new positions. Support counter-attack 4 3rds fired	
	25		Battery relieved X/145	
	26		Battery in action. Inter-battery relief. Ammunition expenditure for the month 402 rds	
	31st		Van Gilder Lt.	

American expenditure for the month 402 rds

Van Gilder Lt.

SECRET

9/11/15

War Diary

of

V/35 Trench Mortar Battery

From 1st Sept'y   To 30th Sept'y

Volume 13

H.E. Walker Capt R.A.
Commanding V/35 Trench Mortar Battery

V/35 "French Mortar Battery, WAR DIARY September 1917

Army Form C. 2118.

INTELLIGENCE SUMMARY.
(Erase heading not required.)

Place	Date	Hour	Summary of Events and Information	Remarks and references to Appendices
18.c.80.40 Sheet 36c	1st		Battery in action at F.11.d.30.45 and F.18.a.10.30.	
	2nd	9-10pm	Trench mortars in action at EAGLE Q.Y. X.29.a.25.25. Shot by 2 S.E Gunner over from 4/62 French Mortar Battery.	
	3rd		2/Lt D.H. URQUHART. R.F.A joined at Strength (Seek in England) Battery in action. No special operations.	
	4th			
	5th			
	6th			
	7th			
	8th		15 rounds expended in support of offensive operation.	
	9th		Nothing to report.	
	10th		3 rds expended during organized shoot on enemy trenches	
	11th		Battery not in action. No special operations.	
	12th			
	13th		11 rds expended during organized night shoot on enemy trenches	
	14th	6.230p	Battery in action, no special operations. 28 rounds expended in retaliation.	
			Battery fired in support of raid on enemy trenches at 10.25 p.m. No rounds expended	
			Battery in action. Normal firing in enemy trenches and trench mortars in retaliation. Expenditure 30 rds	
	25th to 30th		Expenditure for the month 152 rounds. No casualties.	

SECRET

War Diary

of

X/35 Trench Mortar Battery

From 1st Sept 17   To 30th Sept 17

Volume 15

Jas. G. Whitehead. Lieut
Commanding X/35 Trench Mortar Battery

X/36 Trench Mortar Battery

WAR DIARY

September 1919

INTELLIGENCE SUMMARY.
(Erase heading not required.)

Place	Date	Hour	Summary of Events and Information	Remarks and references to Appendices
E.18.c.60.50	1st & 2nd		Battery in action at F.12.c.50.75. 5.1" mor. Intermittent retaliation fire. Hostile shelling yr.	
	3rd		Battery relieved by 48" mor. By. yr.	
	4th		Battery employed on covering parties. yr.	
	5/10 V.		Battery relieved 2/25 Inf. Bg. in line yr.	
	11 Vr.		Battery relieved. Nothing to report. yr.	
	12 V		In action. Nothing to report. yr.	
	13 Vr.		3 rounds expended in reply to hostile fire yr.	
	14 Vr.		Nothing to report. yr.	
	1:25		Battery relieved by 2/25 Inf. Bg. yr.	
	16 Vr. } 21 V. }		Battery employed on covering parties and communication carrying. yr.	
	22 V.		Battery relieved 2/3" mor Bg in line. No issues. yr.	
	23 V.		In action. It was reported yr.	
	28 V.		Relieved by Y.55 mor Bg. yr.	
	29 V.		Nothing to report. yr.	
	30 V.		Ammunition expended during the month: 9 rounds. yr.	

Ja. W. Wilson
Commanding X/36 Tr By.

SECRET

War Diary

of

V/35 Trench Mortar Battery

From 1st Sept 17   To 30th Sept 17

Volume 15

E.W.R. Fitzgerald
Capt:
for Officer Commanding V/35 Trench Mortar Battery
T.M.B. 35th Div

Y/35 Trench Mortar Battery — September 1919

Army Form C. 2118.

WAR DIARY
or
INTELLIGENCE SUMMARY.
(Erase heading not required.)

Place	Date	Hour	Summary of Events and Information	Remarks and references to Appendices
E.18.c.80.50 Sheet 62c	1st		Nothing to report.	E.W.R.?
	2nd		Battery relieved X/35 Embay in line at 7.18.c.80.75. 3rd relieved	E.W.R.?
	3rd			E.W.R.?
	H.Q. 6.0.d.		Battery in action. No inspections. 10 rds expended.	E.W.R.?
	4th		Battery relieved by Y/35 EmBey. 2 Lt C.A. HARRIS 14th Glos Regt arrived to join.	E.W.R.?
	5th to 7th		Battery employed on cooking parties.	E.W.R.?
	8th to 14th			E.W.R.?
	15th		Battery relieves X/35 EmBey in line.	E.W.R.?
	16th 6.8.d.		In action. No operations. 3 rds expended in retaliation.	E.W.R.?
	19th		Relieved by Y/35 EmBey. 2 rds expended.	E.W.R.?
	19th			E.W.R.?
	6.24.c.		Battery employed in cooking parties.	E.W.R.?
	28th		Lt G.H. PULFORD R.F.A. proceeded to China Army School on mortar for Lewis Gun course.	E.W.R.?
	29th		Battery relieves X/35 Y.m Bty in line. 14 men unknown.	E.W.R.?
	30th		In action. Nothing to report. 2 rds expended. Ammunition expended from the month to amount. Casualties Nil.	E.W.R.?

E.W.R. McGrath
Major O.C. Y/35 Trench Mortar Bty.

SECRET

War Diary

of

X/33 Trench Mortar Battery

From 1st Sept 17.   To 30th Sept 17.

Volume 15

E.W.R. Lilywhite Capt.
     L.N.C. 35 th Div.
for Officer Commanding X/33 Trench Mortar Battery

Army Form C. 2118.

2nd Trench Mortar Battery   September 1917

WAR DIARY
or
INTELLIGENCE SUMMARY
(Erase heading not required.)

Instructions regarding War Diaries and Intelligence Summaries are contained in F. S. Regs., Part II. and the Staff Manual respectively. Title pages will be prepared in manuscript.

Place	Date	Hour	Summary of Events and Information	Remarks and references to Appendices
E.18.c.80.50 Sheet 62c	1.9.17 to 7.9.17		Battery employed on working parties	EuR7.
	7th	y.d.	Battery relieves V/35 T.m.Bty in line	EuR7.
	8th to 10th	8h	In action. No special operations. 12 rounds expended in retaliation to hostile fire.	EuR7.
	11th		Battery relieved by X/35 T.m.Bty	EuR7.
	12th to 18th	12d	Battery employed on working parties	EuR7.
	19th		Battery relieves V/35 T.m.Bty in line	EuR7.
	20th	20h	In action. No special operations. & ran down in	EuR7.
	22nd	22nd	10 rounds expended in support of raid on enemy trenches	EuR7.
	25th	25d	Battery relieved by X/35 T.m.Bty	EuR7.
	26th to 30th	20d 6.30h	Battery employed on working parties	EuR7. EuR7.
			Ammunition expended during tour for the month 33 rounds.	EuR7.
			Casualties Nil	

EwR. Stephens Capt
O/m O 2/ Sub sections
for O.C. 2/35 Trench Mortar Battery

SECRET.

War Diary

of

V/35 Trench Mortar Battery

From 1st October 1917   To 31st Octo 1917

Volume 14

EWR Fitz[illegible] Capt
O.C. V/35 Trench Mortar Bty

Army Form C. 2118.

V/35 Trench Mortar Battery   WAR DIARY   October 1919

INTELLIGENCE SUMMARY.
(Erase heading not required.)

Place	Date	Hour	Summary of Events and Information	Remarks and references to Appendices
E.18.c.80.50 Sheet 6×c.	1st		Battery in action, with mortars at F.11.d.30.48 and F.18.c.10.50 (Sheet 6×e), and N.29.d.4.5.35 (Sheet 5×b). No operations.	EWR7
— " —	2nd		Battery in action, no operations	EWR7
— " —	3rd		Battery relieved by V/56 T.M.B.y.	EWR7
— " —	4th		Battery moved by motor lorries to billets in AVESNES-LE-COMTE	EWR7
AVESNES-LE-COMTE	5th to 12th		Battery training in XVII Corps Area (AVESNES-LE-COMTE)	EWR7
ERTINGHEM	13th		Battery proceeded to new billets in ERINGHEM area. The move being made as follows: marched to entraining at AUBIGNY, detrained at ESQUELBECQ, and by motor lorries to ERINGHEM.	EWR7
	14th 15th to 16th		Nothing to report	EWR7
B.10.c.60.40 Sheet 28c BELGIUM	17th		Battery moved by motor lorries to B.10.c.60.40. (Sheet 28) 1000 yds E. of ELVERDINGHE BELGIUM.	EWR7
— " —	18th		Nothing to report	EWR7
— " —	19th		CAPT. H.E. WALLER R.F.A. admitted to hospital, sick. Railway employed on Divisional Ammunition dumps	EWR7
— " —	20th		Battery employed on Ammunition dumps	EWR7
B.13.a.40.40 Sheet 28 BELGIUM	21st		Battery moved to B.13.a.40.40 (Sheet 28 BELGIUM)	EWR7
— " —	22nd to 31st		Work on ammunition dumps continued	EWR7

Ammunition Expenditure for month nil

— EWR7 2½" front trap
0.0 V/35 Trench Mortar Battery
Landed in Nal

SECRET

War Diary

of

X/35 Trench Mortar Battery

From 1st October 1917   To 31st October 1917

Volume 16

J. Matthews Lieut
O.C. X/35 Trench Mortar Battery

X/35 Trench Mortar Battery — October 1917

WAR DIARY
or
INTELLIGENCE SUMMARY
(Erase heading not required.)

Army Form C. 2118.

Place	Date	Hour	Summary of Events and Information	Remarks and references to Appendices
E.18.c.80.40 Sheet 51b	1st		Battery in action at F.18.c.50.45 (Sheet 51b) 3 rds expended	
— " —	3rd		Battery relieved by X/55 Trench mortar Battery	
AVESNES-LE-COMTE	4th		Battery proceeded by motor lorries to AVESNES-LE-COMTE	
— " —	5th		Party of 1 officer and 4 NCOs proceed to II Army School of mortars for instruction on 6" NEWTON mortar	
— " —	6th to 12th		Remainder of Battery carrying out training	
— " —	13th		Party return from II Army School of mortars	
ERINGHEM	14th		Battery proceeded to AUBIGNY, and entrained. Detrained at ESQUELBECQ and proceeded by motors to billets at ERINGHEM	
— " —	15th 16th		Nothing to report	
B.10.c.00.40 Sheet 28 BELGIUM	17th		Moved by motor lorries to B.10.c.00.40 (Sheet 28) 1000 yds E of ELVERDINGHE	
— " —	18th		Nothing to report	
— " —	19th		Battery employed taking ammunition to Battery (Field) positions	
— " —	20th		Battery employed on ammunition carrying	
B.13.a.70.40 Sheet 28 BELGIUM	21st		Moved to B.13.a.70.40 (Sheet 28 BELGIUM)	
— " —	22nd		Battery employed on ammunition carrying parties. 1 O.R. killed	
— " —	23rd to 31st		Work on divisional ammunition dumps continued	

Ammunition expenditure for month 3rds
Casualties 1 O.R. killed

J. Philbin
O.C. X/35 Trench mortar Battery

SECRET

War Diary

of

Y/35 Trench Mortar Battery

From 1st October 1917   To 31st October 1917

Volume 16

C W Raeford
O.C. Y/35 Trench Mortar Battery

WAR DIARY
INTELLIGENCE SUMMARY

War Trench Mortar Battery　　October 1917　　Army Form C. 2118.

Instructions regarding War Diaries and Intelligence Summaries are contained in F.S. Regs., Part II. and the Staff Manual respectively. Title pages will be prepared in manuscript.

(Erase heading not required.)

Place	Date	Hour	Summary of Events and Information	Remarks and references to Appendices
E.18.c.80.50 Sheet 62c	1st		Battery moved to PERONNE	enl
PERONNE	2nd		Battery entrained at PERONNE	enl
AVESNES-LE-COMTE	3rd	4pm	Detrained at AUBIGNY and moved to billets in AVESNES-LE-COMTE	enl
-"-	4th		Nothing to report	enl
-"-	5th		Party of 2 Officers and 4 N.C.Os. proceeded to III Army School of instruction on 6" NEWTON mortar	enl
-"-	6th to 9th		Remainder of Battery carry out training	enl
-"-	10th		Party returns from III Army School of mortars	enl
-"-	12th			enl
-"-	13th		Battery proceeded to AUBIGNY and entrained	enl
ERINGHEM	14th		Detrained at ESQUELBECQ and proceeded by motor lorries to billets at ERINGHEM	enl
-"-	15th to 16th		Nothing to report	enl
B.10.c.60.40 Sheet 28 BELGIUM	17th		Moved to B.10.c.60.40 (Sheet 28 BELGIUM) 1000 yds E of ELVERDINGHE	enl
-"-	18th		Nothing to report	enl
-"-	19th & 20th		Battery employed on ammunition carrying parties for Divisional Ammunition Dumps	enl
B.13.A.70.70 Sheet 28	21st to 27th		Battery employed on Divisional Ammunition Dumps	enl
-"-	28th		Lt. C.W. PULFORD R.F.A. rejoins after extended course at III Army School of mortars. Work on ammunition dumps continues	enl
-"-	29th to 30th		Work on ammunition dumps continues	enl

(A7932). Wt. W2889/M1293. 75,000. 4/17. D.D. & L., Ltd. Forms/C.2118/4.

Ammunition expenditure for month Nil. (x)

C.W. Pulford Lt. R.F.A.
O.C. Y/55 Trench Mortar Battery

SECRET

War Diary

of

Z/35 Trench Mortar Battery

From 1st Octo 1917   To 31st Octo 1917

Volume 16

E.W.R. Fitzgerald Capt.
for
O.C. Z/35 Trench Mortar Bty

Army Form C. 2118.

WAR DIARY — October 1917

INTELLIGENCE SUMMARY.

(Erase heading not required.)

Instructions regarding War Diaries and Intelligence Summaries are contained in F. S. Regs., Part II. and the Staff Manual respectively. Title pages will be prepared in manuscript.

Place	Date	Hour	Summary of Events and Information	Remarks and references to Appendices
E.18.c.80.50 Sheet 62C PERONNE	1st		Battery moved to PERONNE	EWR 7
PERONNE	2nd		Battery entrained at PERONNE	EWR 7
AVESNES LE-COMTE	3rd		Detrained at AUBIGNY and moved to billets in AVESNES-LE-COMTE	EWR 7
— " —	4th		Nothing to report	EWR 7
— " —	5th		Party of 1 Officer and 4 N.C.O.s proceeded to III Army School of mortars for instruction on 6" Newton mortar	EWR 7
— " —	6th & 7th		Battery carrying out training	EWR 7
— " —	12th		Party returns from III Army School of mortars	EWR 7
— " —	13th		Battery proceeded to AUBIGNY also entrained. Detrained at ESQUELBECQ and proceeded by motor lorries to billets at ERINGHEM	EWR 7
ERINGHEM	14th			
— " —	15th & 16th		Nothing to report	EWR 7
B.10.c.60.40 Sheet 28 BELGIUM	17th		Moved to B.10.c.60.40 (Sheet 28) 1000 yds E of ELVERDINGHE	EWR 7
— " —	18th		Nothing to report	EWR 7
— " —	19th & 20th		Battery employed on ammunition carrying carried 10 rs ammunition	EWR 7
B.13.A.70.70 Sheet 28	21st		Moved to B.13.A.70.70 (Sheet 28 BELGIUM)	EWR 7
— " —	22nd to 31st		Work on Divisional Ammunition Dumps continued	EWR 7

Ammunition Expenditure for month nil.
Ammunition Expenditure: for 6 x Z/38 French mortar battery, E.W.R. B/L musketry, for 6 x Z/38 French mortar battery

A.8831—Wt. W4973/M637 750,000 8/16 D.D.& L. Ltd. Forms/C.2118/13.

SECRET.

War Diary

of

V/35 Trench Mortar Battery

From 1st Nov. 1917   To 30th Nov. 1917

Volume 15

E.W.R. Fitzgerald Capt. & T.M.O. 35 Div
for O.C. V/35 Trench Mortar Battery

Army Form C. 2118.

V/35 Trench Mortar Bty.   November 1917

WAR DIARY
or
INTELLIGENCE SUMMARY
(Erase heading not required.)

Instructions regarding War Diaries and Intelligence Summaries are contained in F. S. Regs., Part II. and the Staff Manual respectively. Title pages will be prepared in manuscript.

Place	Date	Hour	Summary of Events and Information	Remarks and references to Appendices
B.13.A.70.70 Sheet 28	1st to 2nd		Battery employed as working parties on dial. Ammunition Dumps	V.W.R.7.
"	3rd		Lieut (acty Capt) H.E. WALLER struck off strength, evacuated sick to England 24.10.14.	V.W.R.7.
"	4th to 9th		Work on Ammunition Dumps continues.	V.W.R.7.
"	10th		Battery employed salving ammunition	V.W.R.7.
"	10th to 14th			V.W.R.7.
B.9.C.00.40 Sheet 28	15th		Moved to B.9.C.00.40 Sheet 28	V.W.R.7.
"	16th to 2nd		Battery employed salving ammunition and guns	V.W.R.7.
"	22nd		2nd T.A.G.K.S. JONES posted from Base. to arts continues	V.W.R.7.
"	23rd		2nd Lt. P.M. LECKIE posted to 157th Brigade R.F.A. Work continued.	V.W.R.7.
"	24th to 24th		Battery employed salving guns	V.W.R.7.
"	28th 29th		Nothing to report	V.W.R.7.
"	30th		Battery employed salving ammunition	V.W.R.7.
			Ammunition expenditure for this month – Nil	V.W.R.7.
			Casualties – Nil	

V.W.R. Fitzgerald Capt
for O.C. V/35 Trench Mortar Battery

(A7992). Wt. W12839/M1293. 75,000. 4/17. D. D. & L., Ltd. Forms/C.2118-14.

Army Form C. 2118.

WAR DIARY
or
INTELLIGENCE SUMMARY.
(Erase heading not required.)

Instructions regarding War Diaries and Intelligence Summaries are contained in F. S. Regs., Part II. and the Staff Manual respectively. Title pages will be prepared in manuscript.

Place	Date	Hour	Summary of Events and Information	Remarks and references to Appendices

SECRET

<u>War Diary</u>

<u>of</u>

<u>X/35 Trench Mortar Battery</u>

<u>From 1st Nov.17.</u>   <u>To 30th Nov.17.</u>

<u>Volume 17</u>

<u>J. H. Whitham.   Lt.</u>
<u>X/35 Trench Mortar Battery</u>

X/35 Trench Mortar Battery

November 1914

INTELLIGENCE SUMMARY.

(Erase heading not required.)

Place	Date	Hour	Summary of Events and Information	Remarks and references to Appendices
B.13.a.70.70. Sheet 28	1st & 9th	9th.) 10.10d.) to 14d.)	Battery employed as working parties on 6in Ammunition Dumps J.H.W. Battery employed salving ammunition J.H.W.	
B.9.c.00.40. Sheet 28	15 do. 16 do. to 18d.		moved to B.9.c.00.40. Shell 28 J.H.W. Battery employed salving guns and ammunition J.H.W.	
"	19 do.		Battery proceeding to 5 th Army Trench Mortar School VALHEUREUX J.H.W.	
VALHEUREUX	20 do. to 30 do.		Battery undergoing instruction on the 6" NEWTON Trench Mortar J.H.W.	

Ammunition expenditure for the month - nil
Casualties nil.

J.H. Watkins. Lt.
X/35 Trench Mortar Battery

Army Form C. 2118.

WAR DIARY
or
INTELLIGENCE SUMMARY.
(Erase heading not required.)

Instructions regarding War Diaries and Intelligence Summaries are contained in F. S. Regs., Part II. and the Staff Manual respectively. Title pages will be prepared in manuscript.

Place	Date	Hour	Summary of Events and Information	Remarks and references to Appendices

(A7692). Wt. W12859/M1293. 75,000. 1/17. D. D. & L., Ltd. Forms/C.2118/14.

SECRET

War Diary

of

Y/35 Trench Mortar Battery

From 1st Nov 17   To 30th Nov 17

Volume 17

C.W. Pulford Lieut RFA
Y/35 Trench Mortar Battery

Army Form C. 2118.

V/35 Trench Mortar Battery

November 1917

WAR DIARY
or
INTELLIGENCE SUMMARY
(Erase heading not required.)

Place	Date	Hour	Summary of Events and Information	Remarks and references to Appendices
B.12.a.90.40 Sheet 28	1st	noon to 9pm	Battery employed as working parties on Div. Ammunition Dumps (3 other ranks wounded)	Cas)
"	"	10.30 to 11.30	Work continued	
"	"	10.30 to 11.30	Battery employed salving ammunition	Cas)
B.9.c.00.40 Sheet 28		10.30	moved to B.9.c.00.40. Sheet 28	Cas)
"		10 am to 2 pm	Battery employed salving guns and ammunition	Cas)
"		20 to noon	Nothing to report.	Cas)
"		30	Battery salving ammunition	Cas)
			Ammunition Expenditure for this month. Nil.	Cas)
			Casualties - 3 other ranks wounded.	

Geo Preston Lt. R.F.A.
V/35 Y Trench Mortar Battery

Army Form C. 2118.

WAR DIARY
or
INTELLIGENCE SUMMARY.
(Erase heading not required.)

Instructions regarding War Diaries and Intelligence Summaries are contained in F. S. Regs., Part II. and the Staff Manual respectively. Title pages will be prepared in manuscript.

Place	Date	Hour	Summary of Events and Information	Remarks and references to Appendices

SECRET

War Diary

of

Z/35 Trench Mortar Battery

From 1st Nov 17   To 30th Nov 17

Volume 17

[signature]
Z/35 Trench Mortar Battery

Z/55 Trench Mortar Battery — November 1917 — Army Form C. 2118.

WAR DIARY
or
INTELLIGENCE SUMMARY.
(Erase heading not required.)

Place	Date	Hour	Summary of Events and Information	Remarks and references to Appendices
B.13.a.70.70. Sheet 28	1.11.17	9th	Battery employed as working parties on Red Ammunition Dumps. N.Q.	
"	10th		Battery employed salving ammunition. N.Q.	
—			moved to B.9.c.00.40. Sheet 28. N.Q.	
B.9.c.00.40. Sheet 28	16th (a 29th)		Battery employed salving guns and ammunition. N.Q.	
	2nd (6 29th)		Nothing to report. N.Q.	
	30th		Employees salving ammunition. N.Q.	
			Ammunition expenditure for the month — nil	
			Casualties — nil.	

W. Dawney
Z/55 Trench Mortar Battery.

Army Form C. 2118.

WAR DIARY
or
INTELLIGENCE SUMMARY.

(Erase heading not required.)

Instructions regarding War Diaries and Intelligence Summaries are contained in F. S. Regs., Part II. and the Staff Manual respectively. Title pages will be prepared in manuscript.

Place	Date	Hour	Summary of Events and Information	Remarks and references to Appendices

(A7692). Wt. W12839/M1293. 75,000. 1/17. D. D. & L., Ltd. Forms/C.2118.14.

Army Form C. 2118.

WAR DIARY
or
INTELLIGENCE SUMMARY.

(*Erase heading not required.*)

Instructions regarding War Diaries and Intelligence Summaries are contained in F. S. Regs., Part II. and the Staff Manual respectively. Title pages will be prepared in manuscript.

Place	Date	Hour	Summary of Events and Information	Remarks and references to Appendices

(A7093). Wt. W12839/M1293. 75,000. 1/17. D. D. & L., Ltd. Forms/C.2118.14.

SECRET.

War Diary

of

V/35 Trench Mortar Battery

From 1st Dec. 1917.   To 31st Dec. 1917

Volume 10

A. G. S. Jones
for O.C. V/35 Trench Mortar Battery

WAR DIARY
INTELLIGENCE SUMMARY.

V/35 Trench Mortar Battery December 1917

Army Form C. 2118.

Place	Date	Hour	Summary of Events and Information	Remarks and references to Appendices
B.9.c.0.4.0 Sheet 28	1st		Battery employed salving ammunition. Lt. C.W. PULFORD, M.C., R.F.A. posted to command V/35 Trench Mortar Battery vice 2ndLt (A/Capt) H.E. WALLER. R.F.A. sick to England.	A.9.S.S. 24.10.17 A.9.S.S.
"	2nd		Work continued. 2ndLt. KASEVILLE R.F.A. posted from Base.	A.9.S.S.
"	3rd to 8th		Battery employed salving ammunition	A.9.S.S.
"	9th		Battery relieved by V/57 Trench Mortar Battery, and proceeded to PERA CAMP E.15 & 5.5 Sheet 27	A.9.S.S.
PERA CAMP E.15 & 5.5 Sheet 27	10th to 12th		Battery training	A.9.S.S.
LEDRINGHEM	13th		Battery moved to billets in LEDRINGHEM	A.9.S.S.
"	14th		Nothing to report	A.9.S.S.
"	15th to 31st		Battery arranging scheme of training	A.9.S.S.

Ammunition expenditure for the month. Nil
Casualties Nil

A.G.S. Gunn 2/Lt. R.F.A.
V/35 Trench Mortar Battery

SECRET

War Diary

of

X/35 Trench Mortar Battery

From 1st Dec. 1914   To 31st Dec 1914

Volume 18

S. Barraclough. Lt.

for OC X/35 Trench Mortar Battery

Army Form C. 2118.

X/35 Trench Mortar Battery   December 1917

WAR DIARY
or
INTELLIGENCE SUMMARY.
(Erase heading not required.)

Instructions regarding War Diaries and Intelligence Summaries are contained in F. S. Regs., Part II. and the Staff Manual respectively. Title pages will be prepared in manuscript.

Place	Date	Hour	Summary of Events and Information	Remarks and references to Appendices
VALHEUREUX	1st		Battery undergoing instruction in 6" Newton Mortar at Fourth Army Trench Mortar School	S.B.
"	2nd		Instruction continued. 2nd Lt. M.A.H. TINCKER R.F.A. posted from 15 Batt. 2nd Lt. S. BARRACLOUGH R.F.A. posted to command X/35 Trench Mortar Battery	S.B.
"	3rd to 12th		Instruction continued	S.B.
"	13th		Battery proceeding by railway to ARNEKE	S.B.
ARNEKE	14th		Battery detrained and billeted at ARNEKE	S.B.
LEDRINGHEM	15th		Battery proceeded to billets at LEDRINGHEM	S.B.
"	16th to 31st		Battery undergoing scheme of training	S.B.
			Ammunition expenditure for the month Nil.	
			Casualties Nil	

S. Barraclough Lt.
X/35 Trench Mortar Battery

SECRET

War Diary

of

V/35 Trench Mortar Battery

From 1st Dec 1917   To 31st Dec 1917

Volume 18

S Barraclough. Lt.
V/35 Trench Mortar Battery

WAR DIARY
INTELLIGENCE SUMMARY

Y/35 Trench Mortar B'y. December 1917. Army Form C. 2118.

Place	Date	Hour	Summary of Events and Information	Remarks and references to Appendices
Bq. 6.00.60. Sheet 28	1st		Battery employed salving ammunition. Lt. C. M. PULFORD M.C. R.F.A. proceeds to command Y/35 Trench Mortar Battery.	SS
"	2nd		Work continued. 2nd Lt. S. BARRACLOUGH R.F.A. posted from X/35 Trench Mortar Battery to command Y/35 Trench Mortar Battery, with rank of Acig. Lieutenant.	SS
"	3rd to 8th		Battery employed salving ammunition.	SS
PERA CAMP E.16.b.5.5. Sheet 27	9th		Battery relieved by Y/59 Trench Mortar Battery and proceeded to PERA CAMP. E.16.b.5.5. Sheet 27	SS
"	10th to 12th		Battery training	SS
LEDRINGHEM	13th		Moved to billets in LEDRINGHEM.	SS
"	14th		Working to renovi.	SS
"	to 15th		Battery proceeding by rail to Fourth Army Trench Mortar School, VAUX-EN-AMIENOIS	SS
VAUX-EN-AMIENOIS	17th to 31st		Battery undergoing instruction on 6" Newton Mortar	SS
			Ammunition expenditure for the month. Nil. Casualties Nil.	SS

S. Barraclough Lt. R.A.
Commanding Y/35 Trench Mortar Battery.

Army Form C. 2118.

WAR DIARY
or
INTELLIGENCE SUMMARY.
(Erase heading not required.)

Instructions regarding War Diaries and Intelligence Summaries are contained in F. S. Regs., Part II. and the Staff Manual respectively. Title pages will be prepared in manuscript.

Place	Date	Hour	Summary of Events and Information	Remarks and references to Appendices

SECRET.

War Diary

of

Z/35 Trench Mortar Battery

From 1st Dec 1917   To 31st Dec 1917

Volume 18

[signature]
Z/35 Trench Mortar Battery Lt.

INTELLIGENCE SUMMARY.

(Erase heading not required.)

Instructions regarding War Diaries and Intelligence Summaries are contained in F.S. Regs., Part II. and the Staff Manual respectively. Title pages will be prepared in manuscript.

Place	Date	Hour	Summary of Events and Information	Remarks and references to Appendices
B.9.c.00.40. Sheet 28	1st		Battery undergoing saluting ammunition. WD.	
	2nd (6.15.h.)		Work continued. 2Lt J.D.TAGGART. M.C. R.F.A. proceed to 18th Bde R.F.A. HQ.	
	2nd (6.6.h.)		Battery employed saluting ammunition WD.	
	9th.		Battery relieved by 2/54 Trench Mortar Battery and moved to PERA CAMP. E 16 10.S.S. Sheet 27. WD.	
PERA CAMP E 16.10.S.S. Sheet 27.	10.do (6.12.h.)		Battery training WD.	
LEDRINGHEM	13.do		Battery moved to billets in LEDRINGHEM WD.	
"	14.do		Finishing its return. WD.	
"	15.do (6.30.h.)		Battery undergoing scheme of training WD.	
"			Ammunition expenditure for the month. Nil WD.	
			Casualties Nil WD.	

B. Cannon Capt.
2/55 Trench Mortar Battery.

SECRET

WAR DIARY

OF

V/35 TRENCH MORTAR BATTERY.

From 1st Jany 1918   To 31st Jany 1918

Volume 17

(signed)
Capt R.A.
Commanding V/35 Trench Mortar Battery

Army Form C. 2118.

V/35 Trench Mortar Battery **WAR DIARY**
or
INTELLIGENCE SUMMARY.

(Erase heading not required.)

January 1918

Place	Date	Hour	Summary of Events and Information	Remarks and references to Appendices
LEDRINGHEM	1st to 9th		Battery undergoing scheme of training	
WELSH FARM	10th		moved to WELSH FARM	
"	11th to 13th		Nothing to report	
C.15.B.2.b. Sheet 28	14th		moved to KEMPTON PARK C.15.B.2.b (Sheet 28) and relieved V/58 Trench mortar Battery, taking over two Heavy trench mortars	
"	15th to 18th		Battery employed on working parties	
"	19th		2/Lt KASEVILLE R.F.A. and 20 other ranks proceed to Senne Army Trench mortar School for course of instruction -	
"	20th		Nothing to report	
"	21st		One Heavy trench mortar taken over from V/39 Trench mortar Battery	
"	22nd to 24th		Battery employed as working parties, salvage, and camp improvement.	
"	25th to 31st		Battery employed as working parties for the 253 Tunnelling Coy.	

Ammunition expenditure for the month - Nil.
Casualties - Nil

J.W.Phelps Capt. R.F.A.
Commanding V/35 Trench mortar Battery

SECRET

WAR DIARY
of
X/35 TRENCH MORTAR BATTERY.

From 1st Jany 1918 To 31st Jany 1918.

Volume 19

J.C. Withas.
                    Lieut
Commanding X/35 Trench Mortar Battery

X/35 Trench Mortar Battery WAR DIARY January 1918

Army Form C. 2118.

INTELLIGENCE SUMMARY
(Erase heading not required.)

Place	Date	Hour	Summary of Events and Information	Remarks and references to Appendices
LEDRINGHEM	1st to 9th		Battery undergoing training.	
WELSH FARM	10th		Moved to WELSH FARM.	
"	11th to 12th		Nothing to report.	
B.28.central Sheet 28	14th		Moved to B.28.central. (Sheet 28) and relieved X/38 Trench Mortar Battery, taking over 4" 6" Newton Trench Mortars.	
"	15th 16th		Nothing to report.	
C.15.B.2.6. Sheet 28	17th		Moved to KEMPTON PARK C.15.B.2.6 (Sheet 28)	
"	18th		Reconnaissance made for 6" Trench mortar position.	
"	19th		Work commenced on emplacement at U.12.D.80.45. Sheet. 20.S.W.	
"	20th to 31st		Work on emplacement continued.	

Ammunition expenditure for the month – Nil
Casualties – Nil

J. A. Walther? Lieut
Commanding X/35 Trench Mortar Battery

SECRET

WAR DIARY

OF

Y/35 TRENCH MORTAR BATTERY

FROM 1ST JANY. 1918   TO 31ST JANY 1918

Volume 10

S Cavaclough L.H. RFA
Commanding X/35 Trench Mortar Battery

Army Form C. 2118.

2/35 Trench Mortar Battery   WAR DIARY   January 1918

INTELLIGENCE SUMMARY.
(Erase heading not required.)

Place	Date	Hour	Summary of Events and Information	Remarks and references to Appendices
LEDRINGHEM	1st (a) 2nd (b)		Battery training	NR.
	3rd (c) to 19th (d)		Battery proceeding by railway to Fourth Army School of Mortars VAUX-EN-AMIENOIS. Battery undergoing instruction on 6" Newton trench mortar at Fourth Army School.	NR. NR. NR.
VAUX-EN-AMIENOIS	3rd (c) to 19th (d)			
	20th		Proceeding by railway	NR.
C.13.b.2.6.	21st		Detrained at POPERINGHE and moved to KEMPTON PARK C.13.b.2.6. (Sheet 28) three 6" Newton trench mortars taken over from 39th 2nd Trench Mortar Battery. Nothing to report.	NR.
	22nd down to 31st		Battery employed as working parties for 2/32 Tunnelling Coy. RE. and on 6" Trench mortar emplacement. Vide J.12.a.80.45 (Sheet 20)	NR. NR.
			Ammunition Expenditure for the month Nil. Casualties Nil	NR. NR.

R. Brown Lieut
2/35 Trench Mortar Battery

SECRET

WAR DIARY

of

V/35 TRENCH MORTAR BATTERY

From 1ST FEBY 1918   To 28th FEBY 1918

Volume 18

Capt R.F.A.
Commanding V/35 Trench Mortar Battery

WAR DIARY / INTELLIGENCE SUMMARY

Army Form C. 2118.

V/55 Trench Mortar Bty.   February 1918

Place	Date	Hour	Summary of Events and Information	Remarks and references to Appendices
KEMPTON PARK C.15.d.2.6. Sheet 28.	1st		Battery, less 2Lt. K.A. SEVILLE and 20 other ranks attending course of instruction at Army Trench Mortar School, employed in working trenches for 283 Tunnelling Coy.	Lost
"	2nd		2/Lt A.G.K.S. JONES proceeded to 2nd Army Trench Mortar School for course of instruction. Work continued.	Lost
"	3rd		2/Lt K.A. SEVILLE and party return from Army Trench Mortar School.	Lost
"	4th to 6th		Work under 283 Tunnelling Coy. continued.	Lost
"	6th		In accordance with G.H.Q. letter N° OB/166 dd. 20.1.18, which renders Heavy Trench Mortar Batteries from one per Division to one per Corps, V/55 Trench Mortar Battery ceased to exist, and CAPT. C.W. PULFORD MC RFA, 2/LEUTS A.G.K.S. JONES and K.A. SEVILLE and R.F.A. R.H. and R.F.A. other ranks being posted to the newly organized X/3 Trench Mortar Battery, and three other ranks to V/II Heavy Trench Mortar Battery. The three 9.45" Trench Mortars in charge were handed over to V/II Trench Mortar Battery.	Lost
			Ammunition expenditure for the month Nil.	
			Casualties Nil.	

B.W. Pulford
Capt. R.F.A.
Commanding V/55 Trench Mortar Battery

SECRET

WAR DIARY

of

X/35 TRENCH MORTAR BATTERY

FROM. 1ST FEBY 1918   TO 28th FEBY 1918

Volume 20.

C.W. Pulford
Capt. R.F.A.
Commanding X/35 Trench Mortar Battery

Army Form C. 2118.

X/35 Trench Mortar Bty. February 1918

WAR DIARY
or
INTELLIGENCE SUMMARY
(Erase heading not required.)

Place	Date	Hour	Summary of Events and Information	Remarks and references to Appendices
KEMPTON PARK C.13 d 2.6 Sheet 28	1st	60.4 Ch	Battery employed constructing 6" Trench Mortar Emplacements at U.12.0. 80.40, U.20.25.10. and U.17. c 35.10.	But
	3rd		Battery re-organized in accordance with G.H.Q. Letter N° 0B/66 dtd 20.1.18., which reduces the number of medium Trench Mortar Batteries per Division from three to two, on an increase in establishment of 4 officers and 53 other ranks, and annexes with 6 Trench Mortars. Of the existing personnel, 2-Lt M.A.H.TINCKER R.F.A and 11 other ranks R.1 and R.F.A were posted to the re-organized Y/35 Trench Mortar Battery, and 10 other ranks R.G.A to V[II] to army Trench Mortar Battery. CAPT C.W.P.-FORD M.C. R.F.A., 2-LTS A.G.K.S. JONES and M.A. SEVILLE and 53 other ranks R.1 and R.F.A were posted from V/35 Trench Mortar Battery, and former the re-organized Battery. Two 2" and two 6" Mortars were taken over from Z/35 Trench Mortar Battery	[sgd]
"	9th 6.30 Ch		Battery employed constructing 6" Trench Mortar Emplacements and Vida Artillery Battery positions.	[sgd]

Ammunition expenditure for the month nil.
Casualties nil.

[signature]
Comm'g X/35 Trench Mortar Battery

Army Form C. 2118.

WAR DIARY
or
INTELLIGENCE SUMMARY

(Erase heading not required.)

Instructions regarding War Diaries and Intelligence Summaries are contained in F. S. Regs., Part II. and the Staff Manual respectively. Title Pages will be prepared in manuscript.

Place	Date	Hour	Summary of Events and Information	Remarks and references to Appendices

2449 Wt. W14957/M90 750,000 1/16 J.B.C. & A. Forms/C.2118/12.

SECRET

WAR DIARY

of

Y/35 TRENCH MORTAR BATTERY

From 1st FEBY 1918   To. 28th FEBY 1918

Volume 20

S Barraclough. Lieut R.F.A.
Commanding Y/35 Trench Mortar Battery

Army Form C. 2118.

425 Trench Mortar Battery WAR DIARY February 1918

INTELLIGENCE SUMMARY

(Erase heading not required.)

Instructions regarding War Diaries and Intelligence Summaries are contained in F. S. Regs., Part II and the Staff Manual respectively. Title Pages will be prepared in manuscript.

Place	Date	Hour	Summary of Events and Information	Remarks and references to Appendices
KEMPTON PARK C.15.B.2.6 Sheet 28	1st (a) 4th		Battery employed registering 6" trench mortar emplacements at U.12.D.80.50, U.12.D.25.10 and U.17.c.35.10. One 6" mortar in action at U.12.D.80.50. One O.R. killed and 1 O.R. wounded	S.S.
	8th		Battery re organized in accordance with G.H.Q. letter No. OB/160 dated No 1.18, which provides the number of medium trench mortar Batteries per Division from three to two, with an increased establishment of 4 Officers and 83 other ranks, armed with six trench mortars. One R.G.A personnel (10 other ranks) moved to VII Army Trench mortar Battery. 2nd Lt. M.A.H. TINCKER R.F.A and 2nd Lt. W.S.CAUVIN and 13 other ranks R.A. and R.F.A. moved from 2/3 Trench mortar Battery. Two 2" mortars and one 6" mortar taken over from 2/3 T.M.B.	S.S.
	9th 10th		Work continued Fired 2 rounds registration on enemy defences	S.S.
	10th		Work continued	S.S.
	11th			S.S.
	13th		Fired 25 rounds in support of raid on enemy trench	S.S.
	16th to 19th		Work continued	S.S.

WAR DIARY or INTELLIGENCE SUMMARY

(Erase heading not required.)

Instructions regarding War Diaries and Intelligence Summaries are contained in F. S. Regs., Part II. and the Staff Manual respectively. Title Pages will be prepared in manuscript.

Place	Date	Hour	Summary of Events and Information	Remarks and references to Appendices
KEMPTON PARK C.15.d.2.6 Sheet 28	20th		Fired 2 rounds registration	S.B.
	21st		Work continued	S.B.
	22nd		Work continued. 1 O.R. wounded.	
	23rd		Work on emplacements continued	S.B.
	to 25th		2/Lt. M.A.H. TINCKER admitted to hospital sick	S.B.
	24th		Fired 8 rounds on S.O.S. lines in reply to enemy bombardment	S.B.
	26th		Fired 12 rounds in support of raid on enemy posts	S.B.
			Lt. W.S. CAUVIN struck off strength - transferred to R.F.C.	
			Ammunition expenditure for the month 47 rounds	
			Casualties 1 O.R. killed 2 O.R. wounded.	

S. Barraclough.
Lieut. R.H.A.
Commanding Y/35. French Mortar Battery

WAR DIARY
or
INTELLIGENCE SUMMARY

(Erase heading not required.)

Instructions regarding War Diaries and Intelligence Summaries are contained in F.S. Regs., Part II and the Staff Manual respectively. Title Pages will be prepared in manuscript.

Place	Date	Hour	Summary of Events and Information	Remarks and references to Appendices

SECRET

WAR DIARY

of

Z/35 TRENCH MORTAR BATTERY

FROM 1ST. FEBY 1918   TO 28TH FEBY 1918

Volume 20

[signature]
Capt. R.F.A.
for O.C. Z/35 Trench Mortar Battery

Z/35 Trench Mortar Battery WAR DIARY February 1918

Army Form C. 2118.

INTELLIGENCE SUMMARY

Place	Date	Hour	Summary of Events and Information	Remarks and references to Appendices
KEMPTON PARK C.15.d.2.6. Sheet 28.	1st to 6th 8th		Battery employed making 6" Trench Mortar Emplacements at U.12.D.80.50., U.12.D.25.10. and U.17.c.35.10, Shell 48. In accordance with G.H.Q. letter O.B./66 dated 10.1.18, making good the number of medium trench mortar Batteries per Division from three to two, Z/35 Trench Mortar Battery ceased to be a unit. LIEUT W.S. CAUVIN and 13 R.H. and R.F.A other ranks being posted to Y/35 Trench Mortar Battery, and 7 R.G.A other ranks to V/II Trench Mortar Battery. The Trench Mortars on charge were handed over as follows: - 2 - 2" and 2 - 6" to X/35 T.M. Bry., and 2 2" and 1.6" to Y/35 T.M. Bry. Ammunition expenditure for the month Nil. Casualties Nil.	[sgd?] [sgd?] [sgd?]

[signature] B.S. Prieto?
for O.C. Z/35 Trench Mortar Battery
loans R.Y.A.
Trench Mortar Battery

Army Form C. 2118.

WAR DIARY
or
INTELLIGENCE SUMMARY

(Erase heading not required.)

Instructions regarding War Diaries and Intelligence Summaries are contained in F. S. Regs., Part II. and the Staff Manual respectively. Title Pages will be prepared in manuscript.

Place	Date	Hour	Summary of Events and Information	Remarks and references to Appendices

2449 Wt. W14957/M90 750,000 1/16 J.B.C. & A. Forms/C.2118/12.

35th Div.

WAR DIARY

X/35 TRENCH MORTAR BATTERY.

M A R C H

1 9 1 8

Y/35 Trench Mortar Battery **WAR DIARY** of January 1918

Army Form C. 2118.

INTELLIGENCE SUMMARY.
(Erase heading not required.)

Place	Date	Hour	Summary of Events and Information	Remarks and references to Appendices
VAUX-EN-AMIÉNOIS	1st to 4th		Battery undergoing instruction at Fourth Army Trench Mortar School.	SB
	5th		Proceeding by train	SB
LEDRINGHEM	6 do		Detrained at ARNEKE and moved to billets at LEDRINGHEM	SB
"	7th do (9th)		Nothing to report.	SB
"	10 do		Moved to WELSH FARM	SB
WELSH FARM	11 do (to 13 do)		Nothing to report	SB
B.28 central Sheet 28	14 do		Moved to B.26 central (Sheet 26) relieves Y/58 Trench Mortar Battery taking over three 6" Newton Trench mortars	SB
"	15 do (to 17 do)		Nothing to report.	SB
C.15.b.2.6 Sheet 28.	18 do		Moved to KEMPTON PARK C.15.b.2.6. (Sheet 28)	SB
"	19 do (to 20 do)		Nothing to report	SB
	21 do		One 6" Newton Trench Mortar taken over from 39th Divl. Trench Mortar Bxio	SB
	22 do (to 31 do)		Battery employed as working parties for 253 Tunnelling Coy, and on 6" Trench mortar emplacement at U.12.d.8048 (Sheet 20)	SB
			Ammunition expenditure for the month — Nil	SB
			Casualties — Nil.	SB

S Barraclough Lieut R.g.a.
Commanding Y/35 Trench Mortar Battery

Army Form C. 2118.

X/35 Trench Mortar Battery   March 1918

WAR DIARY or INTELLIGENCE SUMMARY

Vol. 21

(Erase heading not required.)

Instructions regarding War Diaries and Intelligence Summaries are contained in F. S. Regs., Part II. and the Staff Manual respectively. Title Pages will be prepared in manuscript.

Place	Date	Hour	Summary of Events and Information	Remarks and references to Appendices
E. 15.b. 7.7. Sheet 52 NW	1st to 10th		Battery employed constructing 6" T.M. emplacements at V.13.D.90.30, V.18.a.70.60., V.17.c.25.15 and field artillery positions on Army Line.	Jes. Army Line Jas.
CANAL BANK	11th		Battery relieved by 102nd Divl Trench Mortar Batteries and moved to dug-out in CANAL BANK.	Jas.
do.	12th to 14th		Nothing to report.	Jas.
CROMBEKE	15th		Moved to billets in reserve area at CROMBEKE	Jas.
do.	16th to 23rd		Battery training in reserve area.	Jas.
	24th		Entrained at PROVEN and detrained at HEILLY. Marched to billets at CHIPILLY.	Jas.
CHIPILLY	25th		Nothing to report.	Jas.
			Moved to HENNENCOURT.	Jas.
HENNENCOURT	26th			
WARLOY	27th		Moved to WARLOY. Battery employed on marking parties and	Jes.
	28th 29th		ammunition dumps. Work continued. 2/Lt. A.G.K.S. JONES detached for duty (temp.) with 79th Bde. R.F.A.	Jes.
do. 13.a. near 6.20.	30th		Moved to camp in C.13.a. Sheet 62D (near) BETHENCOURT	Jes.
do.	31st		Battery employed on field ammunition dumps.	Jes.

Casualties for the month nil. Jas.

Jas. E. Whitehead Lt.
O.C. X/35 Trench Mortar Battery

35th Div.

Y/35 TRENCH MORTAR BATTERY.

M A R C H

1 9 1 8

DIARY

SECRET

WAR DIARY

OF

Y/35 TRENCH MORTAR BATTERY

From 1ST MARCH 1918 To 31ST MARCH 1918

Volume 21

Barraclough Lieut R.F.A
Commanding Y/35 Trench Mortar Battery

Army Form C. 2118.

V35 Trench Mortar Battery WAR DIARY March 1918 Vol. 21.

or

INTELLIGENCE SUMMARY

(Erase heading not required.)

Instructions regarding War Diaries and Intelligence Summaries are contained in F. S. Regs., Part II. and the Staff Manual respectively. Title Pages will be prepared in manuscript.

Place	Date	Hour	Summary of Events and Information	Remarks and references to Appendices
C.15.b.7.7. Sheet 28 N.W.	1st	1.00	Battery in action, with 6" T.M's at J.B.2.a.8.3. J.13.2.a0.3.5 and U.12.d.3.50. 2-7 A.E WINN S.B	SB
	2nd		R.F.A. front being relieved from this date with effect from 27.2.18	SB
	3rd		Battery in action	SB
	4th		2.Lt. H.T. CROSSLEY R.F.A. joined, being posted from 55 D.A.C.	SB
	10th		Battery in action. No enemy aeroplanes	
CANAL BK	11th		Section relieved by 1st Devon Trench Mortar Bty, and marched to billets in CANAL BANK.	SB
DO	12th) to 14th)		Nothing to report	SB
CROMBEKE	15th		Battery moved to billets in reserve area at CROMBEKE	SB
do	16th to 22nd		Battery training in reserve area	SB
	23rd		Entrained at PROVEN	SB
CHIPILLY	24th		Detrained at HEILLY and marched to CHIPILLY	
HENNENCOURT	25th		Moved to HENNENCOURT	
WARLOY	26th		Moved to WARLOY	
"	28th		2.Lt. O.R. HARRIS and party of men commenced construction of pits 6" T.M. emplacements at E.19.D.O.B. Sheet 62.D.	SB
"	30th		Expdy Commander 2.Lt. ARMINN and H.T. CROSSLEY decided from study (empty) with 159 Inf Bde G.H.Q.	73
C.13.C. Sheet O.2.D.	Coop.		Wire commenced. Remainder of Battery proceed to camp at C.13.a. Sheet 62.D	73
	31st		Work continued	SB

Ammunition expenditure for the month NIL. Casualties NIL. Honours NIL.

J.Shawcaluyh Lieut R.F.A.
Commanding V35

SECRET

WAR DIARY

OF

X/35 TRENCH MORTAR BATTERY.

From. 1st April 1918 — To 30th April 1918.

Volume 22.

J.G. Whitbas. Capt.
Commanding X/35 Trench Mortar Battery

Y/35 Trench Mortar Battery WAR DIARY / INTELLIGENCE SUMMARY April 1918 Army Form C. 2118.

Place	Date	Hour	Summary of Events and Information	Remarks and references to Appendices
C.12 central Sheet 62d	1st		Nothing to report	Yes
PONT NOYELLES	2nd		Moved to PONT NOYELLES	Yes
PONT NOYELLES	3rd & 4th & 5th & 6th		Employed on building Ammunition Dumps	Yes
BRESLE	7th		Moved to BRESLE and relieved Y/35 T.M.Bry in action with 2-6" T.M's at E.25.a.2.8.	Yes
	8th		In action. No special operations. Fired 38 rounds registration rounds.	Yes
	to 11th		on enemy defences	Yes
PONT NOYELLES	12th		Relieved by Third AUST. DIVN. T.M. Bries. and moved to PONT NOYELLES	Yes
HERRISART	13th		Moved to HERRISART	Yes
WARLOY	14th		Moved to WARLOY	Yes
	15th to 19th		Constructing 6" T.M. reserve positions in V.18.a. and V.12.a. Sheet 57d.	Yes
SENLIS	20th		Moved to SENLIS, and relieved Y/35.T.M.Bry in line, with mortars at W.3.c.10.65. W.3.c.10.40. W.3.c.09.95 and W.3.a.9.5.65. 1 O.R. wounded.	Yes
	21st to 22nd		In action. Fired 11 rounds	Yes
	23rd		Fired 122 rounds on enemy defences in support of infantry	Yes
	to 26th		In action. Fired 28 rounds on AVELUY WOOD	Yes
V.I.C.2.D.	27th		Relieved by Y/35 T.M.Bry and moved to V.1.c.2.D. Sheet 57.d. CAPT.C.W.PULFORD M.C. appointed D.T.M.O. 35 DIVN. vice CAPT. E.W.R.FITZGERALD M.C. with effect from 5.3.18. LT. J.G.WHITEHEAD appointed to command X/35.T.M.Bry. with effect from 7.3.18.	Yes
	28th		Work on reserve positions continued. 2.LT. H.T. CROSSLEY joined from Y/35.T.M.Bry.	Yes
	29th		Work continued.	Yes
	30th		Work continued. LT. F.R.SMITH R.F.A. posted and joined from Base.	Yes

Ammunition expenditure for the month 199 rounds

Certified correct. Re: appendices
F.H. Whitehead Lieut.
Commanding X/35 Trench Mortar Battery

SECRET

WAR DIARY
OF
Y/35. TRENCH MORTAR BATTERY

FROM 1ST APRIL 1918   TO 31ST APRIL 1918

VOLUME 22

S. Barraclough. Capt. R.F.A.
Commanding Y/35. Trench Mortar Battery.

Instructions regarding War Diaries and Intelligence
Summaries are contained in F.S. Regs., Part II.
and the Staff Manual respectively. Title pages
will be prepared in manuscript.

Army Form C. 2118.

Y/35 Trench Mortar Battery WAR DIARY or INTELLIGENCE SUMMARY.
(Erase heading not required.)

April 1918

Place	Date	Hour	Summary of Events and Information	Remarks and references to Appendices
BRESLE	1st (a)		Battery constructing 6" T.M. emplacements at E.25.a.4.8. Shelled b.v.O	SB
	2nd		2nd/Lt (A/Lt) S.BARRACLOUGH appointed adjutant & bomb which upset from 1.2.18	SB
	4th		Emplacements completed and mortars mounted in position	SB
	5th (a)		Relieved by X/35 T.M.Bty. Moved to PONT NOYELLES	SB
	5th to 6th			SB
PONT NOYELLES	6th		Battery employed on 2nd Ammunition Dump	SB
	8th (a)			SB
	11th			SB
HERRISART	12th		Moved to HERRISART	SB
SENLIS	13th		Relieved X/147 T.M.Bty. in action with 6" T.M.S at W.3.c.14.65. W.3.c.10.70. W.3.a.95.55. headquarters at SENLIS	SB
	14th		In action, no special operations. Fired 25 rounds. 1 other ranks wounded.	SB
	20.19.(a)			SB
WARLOY	20th		Relieved by X/35 T.M.Bty. and moves to WARLOY	SB
	21st		Employed constructing reserve 3" T.M positions in V.12.b. and V.18.a. Shells by a	SB
	22.25(a)			SB
	26th		CAPT O.W.PULFORD M.C. appointed O.T.M.O. 35th DIVN and CAPT E.W.R.FITZGERALD M.C. would effect from 5.8.18	SB
SENLIS	24th		Relieve X/35 T.M.Bty in action. Fired 95 rounds on AVELUY WOOD in support of operation and S.O.S.	SB
	28th		Fired 5 rounds. 2/Lt H.T.CROSSLEY posted to X/35 T.M.Bty	SB
	29th		Fired 10 rounds	SB
	30th		Fired 39 rounds on AVELUY WOOD and enemy trench mortar	SB
			Ammunition expenditure for this month 170 rounds	SB
			Casualties 1 O.R. wounded	SB

S Barraclough
Commanding Y/35 Trench Mortar Battery

SECRET

WAR DIARY
OF
X/35 TRENCH MORTAR BATTERY
FROM 1ST MAY 1918 TO 31ST MAY 1918
VOLUME 23

[signature] Capt
Commanding X/35 Trench Mortar Battery

WAR DIARY
or
INTELLIGENCE SUMMARY.

(Erase heading not required.)

Army Form C. 2118.

WAR DIARY
of
X 55 TRENCH MORTAR BATTERY

FROM 1st MAY 1918 TO 31st MAY 1918

Army Form C. 2118.

WAR DIARY
or
INTELLIGENCE SUMMARY

(Erase heading not required.)

X/35 Trench Mortar Battery   May 1918

Instructions regarding War Diaries and Intelligence Summaries are contained in F.S. Regs., Part II. and the Staff Manual respectively. Title pages will be prepared in manuscript.

Place	Date	Hour	Summary of Events and Information	Remarks and references to Appendices
W.1.C.d.2. Sheet 57d	1st		Battery in reserve, detachments manning reserve positions E of BOUZINCOURT	Ens?
	2nd		Battery in reserve. Take over two 6" trench mortars in action at W.14.b.10.10 and W.14.a.60.b.5. (Sheet 57d) from 8 3rd Div.	Ens?
	3rd		Battery in reserve	Ens?
SENLIS	4th		moved to SENLIS and relieved Y/35 T.M.B. in action, with four 6" T.M.s in W.3.c. (Sheet 57d)	Ens?
	5th		Battery in action, no operations	Ens?
	to 8th			Ens?
	9th		Carry out intermittent bombardment of enemy positions in ravine W.9.a. Sheet 57d. Relieved during evening by Y/35 T.M.B.	Ens?
W.1.C.d.2 Sheet 57d	10th to 13th		Battery in reserve detachments man reserve positions	Ens?
SENLIS	14th		Relieve Y/35. T.M.B. in action	Ens?
	15th		In action. Fire 5 rounds registration	Ens?
	16th		Fire 10 rds. on enemy trench mortar	
	17th		Fire 40 rds. on enemy defences and T.M. registration	Ens?
	18th		Fire 49 rds on enemy ravine in W.9.a. (Sheet 57d) in airplane of in action.	Ens?
	19th		Enemy artillery obtain direct hit on ammunition dump, causing explosion and wounding one N.C.O. 3 o.r.s area in retaliation to hostile shelling attachments man reserve positions Relieved by Y/35 T.M.B.	Ens?
	20th		Battery in reserve	
	21st to 25th			
	26th		Relieve Y/35. in action. Fire 104 rounds in reply to enemy bombardment. 3 other ranks wounded during night.	Ens? post
W.1.C.d.2 SENLIS			2 Lt H.T. CROSSLEY struck off attachment to R.G.A & rejd	Ens?

2 Lt H.T. CROSSLEY

WAR DIARY
or
INTELLIGENCE SUMMARY.

(Erase heading not required.)

Instructions regarding War Diaries and Intelligence Summaries are contained in F. S. Regs., Part II. and the Staff Manual respectively. Title pages will be prepared in manuscript.

Place	Date	Hour	Summary of Events and Information	Remarks and references to Appendices
SENLIS	2nd Nov to 29th		In action, no firing	[ill]
	30th		Expended 25 rounds registration on enemy defences	[ill]
	31st		In action. In wire bombardment at 11.25pm of enemy defences in support of operation	[ill]
			Casualties during month - 4. O.R. wounded.	G.S.R.
			Ammunition expended. 300 rounds	

A.S.Rolfe? Capt.
Commanding X/35. Trench Mortar Battery

WAR DIARY
or
INTELLIGENCE SUMMARY.

(Erase heading not required.)

Instructions regarding War Diaries and Intelligence Summaries are contained in F. S. Regs., Part II. and the Staff Manual respectively. Title pages will be prepared in manuscript.

Place	Date	Hour	Summary of Events and Information	Remarks and references to Appendices

SECRET

WAR DIARY

OF

Y/35 TRENCH MORTAR BATTERY

FROM 1ST MAY 1918 TO 31ST MAY 1918

VOLUME 23

S. Sanderson Capt. R.F.A.
Commanding Y/35 Trench Mortar Battery

WAR DIARY

Army Form C. 2118.

Instructions regarding War Diaries and Intelligence Summaries are contained in F. S. Regs., Part II. and the Staff Manual respectively. Title pages will be prepared in manuscript.

1/55 Trench Mortar Battery

WAR DIARY or INTELLIGENCE SUMMARY

May 1918

(Erase heading not required.)

Place	Date	Hour	Summary of Events and Information	Remarks and references to Appendices
SENLIS	1st		Battery in action with four 6" trench mortars in W.B.a. (Sheet 57D)	AB
	2nd		area in registration	AB
	4th		In action fired 8 rounds. Relieved by X/55 T.M.B. Detachments man reserve positions	AB
	5th			AB
V.I.C.2.d.	6to 8th		Battery in reserve	AB
Sheet 57D	9th		Relieved X/55 T.M.B.	AB
SENLIS	10th		Bombarded enemy defences in support of infantry operation in AVELUY WOOD. 290 rounds expended. Enemy obtained direct hits on emplacement at W.14.b.90.70. (Sheet 57D) destroying trench mortar and killing three and wounding one other ranks.	AB
"	11th		In action, fire 15 rounds	AB
"	12to 13th		Relieved by X/55 T.M.B. Detachments man reserve positions	AB
V.I.C.2.D.	14th			AB
"	15 to ?		Battery in reserve	AB
"	19th		Relieved X/55 T.M.B in action	AB
SENLIS	20th		In action, no operations	AB
"	21st		Bombarded enemy trenches 29 rounds expended on registration and raid by our infantry in W.9.d. (Sheet 57D) in support of raid by our infantry, 62 rounds expended	SB
"	24th		In action, 1 rounds fired	AB
V.I.C.2.2.	25th		Relieved by X/55 T.M.B., and moved into reserve	AB

Army Form C. 2118.

WAR DIARY
or
INTELLIGENCE SUMMARY.

(Erase heading not required.)

Army Form C. 2118.

Instructions regarding War Diaries and Intelligence Summaries are contained in F. S. Regs., Part II. and the Staff Manual respectively. Title pages will be prepared in manuscript.

Place	Date	Hour	Summary of Events and Information	Remarks and references to Appendices
Y.C.2.2. Sheet 57D	31st July 1916		Resting in reserve, with relief units manning reserve positions E. of BOUZINCOURT. Casualties during month — 3 OR killed, 1 OR wounded. Ammunition expended 451 rounds.	

S Barraclough Major RA
Commanding V/55 Trench Mortar Battery

Army Form C. 2118.

WAR DIARY
or
INTELLIGENCE SUMMARY.

(Erase heading not required.)

Instructions regarding War Diaries and Intelligence Summaries are contained in F. S. Regs., Part II. and the Staff Manual respectively. Title pages will be prepared in manuscript.

Place	Date	Hour	Summary of Events and Information	Remarks and references to Appendices

SECRET

WAR DIARY

OF

X/35 TRENCH MORTAR BATTERY

FROM 1ST JUNE 1918   TO 30TH JUNE 1918

Volume 24

J.G. Witham Capt
Commanding X/35 Trench Mortar Battery

Army Form C. 2118.

WAR DIARY
or
INTELLIGENCE SUMMARY.
(Erase heading not required.)

Instructions regarding War Diaries and Intelligence Summaries are contained in F. S. Regs., Part II. and the Staff Manual respectively. Title pages will be prepared in manuscript.

Place	Date	Hour	Summary of Events and Information	Remarks and references to Appendices

1/35 Trench Mortar Battery   June 1918.   Army Form C. 2118.

WAR DIARY
or
INTELLIGENCE SUMMARY.
(Erase heading not required.)

Instructions regarding War Diaries and Intelligence
Summaries are contained in F. S. Regs., Part II.
and the Staff Manual respectively. Title pages
will be prepared in manuscript.

Place	Date	Hour	Summary of Events and Information	Remarks and references to Appendices
SENLIS	1st		Battery in action with six 6" T.M.G. in position in W.5 and W.14. (Sheet 57 D) Fired 180 rds on enemy defences in support of infantry operation	SS
"	2nd		In action. Fired 15 rds registration on AVELUY WOOD	SS
V.18.a.9.1 Thiepval	3rd		Relieved by X/35. T.M.B.Ty and marched reserve position E. of BOUZINCOURT. Remainder of battery moved to camp V.18.d.9.1. (Sheet 57D. SE)	SS
"	4th 5th		Battery in reserve.	SS
SENLIS	6th		Relieved X/35 T.M.B.Ty in action. Fired 30 rds in retaliation to hostile trench mortars, and 10 rds during bombardment of AVELUY WOOD	SS
"	9th		In action. Fired 21 rds on enemy wire in W.15 in preparation for operation	SS
"	10th		In action. Fired 6 rds in reply to hostile trench mortar and 15 rds on enemy wire in W.15. E.	SS
"	11th		In action. Fired 10 rds on enemy defences in AVELUY WOOD and 66 rds on enemy wire and hostile mortars	SS
"	12th		Fired 6 rds	SS
"	13th		Fired 6 rds on hostile mortars. Relieved by X/35. T.M.B.Ty and marched reserve positions	SS

Army Form C. 2118.

WAR DIARY
or
INTELLIGENCE SUMMARY.
(Erase heading not required.)

Place	Date	Hour	Summary of Events and Information	Remarks and references to Appendices
V.18.a.9.1. (Sheet 57A)	1-9-16 2-9-16		Battery in reserve.	
	10th		Relieved by Y/13 Trench Mortar Battery, and proceeded to RAINCHEVAL.	
RAINCHEVAL	19th 30th		Battery in G.H.Q. reserve, and undergoing scheme of training.	
			Ammunition expenditure for the month 500 rounds 10 rounds Rifle	

Stansborough Capt. R.F.A.
Comg Y/35 Trench Mortar Battery

Army Form C. 2118.

WAR DIARY
or
INTELLIGENCE SUMMARY.
(Erase heading not required.)

Instructions regarding War Diaries and Intelligence Summaries are contained in F. S. Regs., Part II. and the Staff Manual respectively. Title pages will be prepared in manuscript.

Place	Date	Hour	Summary of Events and Information	Remarks and references to Appendices

SECRET

WAR DIARY

OF

Y/35 TRENCH MORTAR BATTERY

From. 1st June 1918   To. 30th June 1918

Volume. 24

S Barraclough Capt. R.F.A.
Commanding Y/35 Trench Mortar Battery

X/35 Trench Mortar Bty

WAR DIARY
INTELLIGENCE SUMMARY

Army Form C. 2118.

June 1918

Place	Date	Hour	Summary of Events and Information	Remarks and references to Appendices
V.I.C.2.2. Sheet 57D	1st		Battery in reserve, detachments manning reserve positions E. of BOUZINCOURT	
	2nd		Battery in reserve.	
BENUS	3rd		Battery relieved Y/35 T.M.Bty. in action with six 6" T.M.'s in position in W.3. and W.14. (Sheet 57D) Fired 3 rds registration.	
	4th		In action. Fired 60 rds on enemy trenches and machine guns.	
	5th (to 6th)		In action. No special operations. Fired up no retaliation. 2nd Lt. H PLAYLE joined from 35th Inf. Ammunition Column.	
	7th		Fired 83 rds registration and bombardment of enemy's wire in W.15.d. One O.R. wounded.	
V.18.d.9.1. Sheet 57d	8th		Battery relieved by Y/35 T.M.Bty, and detachments man reserve positions. Remainder of battery proceed to camp V.18.a.9.1. (Sheet 57D)	
	9th to 12th		Battery in reserve.	
SENLIS	13th		Relieved Y/35 T.M.Bty in action and fired 8 rds in retaliation to hostile trench mortars.	
	14th		In action. Fired 42 rds on hostile Trench Mortars.	
	15th		In action. Fired 83 rds in reply to enemy bombardment.	
	16th		In action. One O.R. wounded.	
RAINCHEVAL	17th		Relieved by X/12 Trench Mortar Bty., and proceeded to RAINCHEVAL	

Army Form C. 2118.

WAR DIARY
or
INTELLIGENCE SUMMARY.
(Erase heading not required.)

Instructions regarding War Diaries and Intelligence Summaries are contained in F. S. Regs. Part II. and the Staff Manual respectively. Title pages will be prepared in manuscript.

Place	Date	Hour	Summary of Events and Information	Remarks and references to Appendices
RAINCHEVAL	18th to 30th		Battn. in G.H.Q. reserve, and undergoing progressive scheme of training.	
			Ammunition expended for the month 224 rounds	
			Casualties 2 other ranks wounded	

J.V. W..
Captain
Commanding 1/28 Trench Mortar Battery.

Army Form C. 2118.

WAR DIARY
or
INTELLIGENCE SUMMARY.

(Erase heading not required.)

Instructions regarding War Diaries and Intelligence Summaries are contained in F. S. Regs., Part II. and the Staff Manual respectively. Title pages will be prepared in manuscript.

Place	Date	Hour	Summary of Events and Information	Remarks and references to Appendices

(A10256) Wt ., 5300/P713 750,000 2/16 Sch. 52 Forms/C2118/16 D. D. & L., London, E.C.

SECRET

WAR DIARY
- of -
X/35 TRENCH MORTAR BATTERY

FROM 1ST JULY 1918 to. 31ST JULY 1918

VOLUME 25

S Barraclough Capt. R.F.A.
Commanding X/35 Trench Mortar Battery

Y/25 Trench Mortar Battery   WAR DIARY   July 1918   Army Form C. 2118.

INTELLIGENCE SUMMARY

Place	Date	Hour	Summary of Events and Information	Remarks and references to Appendices
RAINCHEVAL	1st		In reserve. Orders for entraining receive	SB
	2nd		Battery proceeded to DOULLENS and entraining entrained at ARQUE'S and moved to billets at Sheet 27 - J.1.c.2.5	SB
Sheet 27 J.1.c.2.8.	3rd to 7th		Nothing to report	SB
Sheet 27 R7.a.9.9	8th		Moved to Sheet 27 - R.7.a.9.9	SB
"	9th		Lt C.A. HARRIS and party of 20 other ranks detached for work on observation post for 159 Brigade R.F.A.	SB
"	10th to 15th		Remainder of battery employed on Corp Ammunition Refilling Point.	SB
"	16th		Lt. C.A. HARRIS rejoins with 10 other ranks	SB
"	17th		Reconnaissance made for sites for 6" trench mortars and valleys in M.27 - Sheet 28 selected at M.31.a.5.0.12. 2nd Lt A.E. WINN M.C. proceeds to 159th Brigade R.F.A. Lt H.M. MCHIE joins from "Base Depot"	SB
"	18th		Work on positions commenced.	SB
"	10th to 2nd		Work on positions continued, and mortars mounted in positions.	SB
			Ammunition expenditure for the month NIL Casualties NIL	SB SB

S Daraebrigh Major R.F.A.
Commanding Y25 Trench Mortar Battery

Army Form C. 2118.

WAR DIARY
or
INTELLIGENCE SUMMARY.

(Erase heading not required.)

Place	Date	Hour	Summary of Events and Information	Remarks and references to Appendices

Instructions regarding War Diaries and Intelligence Summaries are contained in F. S. Regs., Part II. and the Staff Manual respectively. Title pages will be prepared in manuscript.

D. D. & L., London, E.C.
(A8604) Wt. W1771/M2731 750,000 5/17 **Sch. 52** Forms/C2118/14

SECRET

WAR DIARY

— of —

X/35 TRENCH MORTAR BATTERY

FROM. 1ST JULY 1918 to 31ST JULY 1918

VOLUME 25

[signature] Capt. R.F.A.
for O.C. X/35 Trench Mortar Battery

Army Form C. 2118.

X/5. Trench Mortar Battery   July 1918

WAR DIARY
or
INTELLIGENCE SUMMARY.
(Erase heading not required.)

Instructions regarding War Diaries and Intelligence Summaries are contained in F. S. Regs., Part II. and the Staff Manual respectively. Title pages will be prepared in manuscript.

Place	Date	Hour	Summary of Events and Information	Remarks and references to Appendices
RAINCHEVAL	1st.		In reserve.	
	2nd		Orders for entraining received. Battery proceeded to DOULLENS and entrained. Detrained at ARQUES and moved to billets at Sheet 27 - J.1.c.2.8.	
Sheet 27 J.1.c.2.8	3rd to 7th		Nothing to report.	
Sheet 27 R.7.a.9.9.	8th.		Moved to Sheet 27 - R.7.a.9.9.	
	9th.		Lt F.R.SMITH and party of 20 other ranks detached for work on observation post for 189 Brigade R.F.A.	
"	10th 14th		Remainder of battery temporarily employed on Civil Ammunition Refilling Point for 189 Brigade R.F.A.	
"	15th		Lieuts A.C.K.STONES and H. PLAYLE attached for duty to 189 Brigade R.F.A.	
"	16th		Lt F.R.SMITH returns with 10 other ranks	
"	17th		Reconnaissance made for sites of 6" Trench Mortar positions to cover the valleys and trenches in Sheet 28.- M.28. Sites selected at Sheet 28.- M.22.a.45.40 and M.22.a H.0.36.	
"	18th		Construction of positions commenced.	
"	19th		Work continued.	
"	20th.		Work continued. Lieut. F.R.SMITH proceeds to 35. D.A.C. and Lt R.F SPALDING proceeds from R.F.A. Base Depot. Lt. A.C.K.STONES reports	

Army Form C. 2118.

WAR DIARY
or
INTELLIGENCE SUMMARY.
(Erase heading not required.)

Instructions regarding War Diaries and Intelligence Summaries are contained in F. S. Regs., Part II. and the Staff Manual respectively. Title pages will be prepared in manuscript.

Place	Date	Hour	Summary of Events and Information	Remarks and references to Appendices
R.7.a.9.9 Sheet 27	2nd to 31st		Work on construction of emplacements, &c carried on. Towers moved muzzles in position, and ammunition received.	Cpl
			Ammunition expenditure for the month - Nil.	Cpl
			Casualties - Nil.	
			Bishyford Capt RHA. for O.C. 8/32 Heavy Motor Battery	

D. D. & L., London, E.C.
(A8004) Wt. W1771/M2 31 750,000 5/17 Sch. 52 Forms/C2118/14

Army Form C. 2118.

WAR DIARY
or
INTELLIGENCE SUMMARY.

(Erase heading not required.)

Instructions regarding War Diaries and Intelligence Summaries are contained in F. S. Regs., Part II. and the Staff Manual respectively. Title pages will be prepared in manuscript.

Place	Date	Hour	Summary of Events and Information	Remarks and references to Appendices

D. D. & L., London, E.C.
(A8024) Wt. W1771/M131 750,000 5/17 Sch. 52 Forms/C2118/14

SECRET.

WAR DIARY

— of —

X/35 TRENCH MORTAR BATTERY.

FROM 1st AUGUST   TO 31st AUGUST 1918.

Volume 26

J.T. Wk........ Capt
Commanding X/35 Trench Mortar Battery

Army Form C. 2118.

WAR DIARY
or
INTELLIGENCE SUMMARY.
(Erase heading not required.)

WAR DIARY

— of —

X 23 TRENCH MORTAR BATTERY

from 1st September 1916 to 31st August 1917

Volume 22

Place	Date	Hour	Summary of Events and Information	Remarks and references to Appendices

Instructions regarding War Diaries and Intelligence Summaries are contained in F. S. Regs., Part II. and the Staff Manual respectively. Title pages will be prepared in manuscript.

WAR DIARY or INTELLIGENCE SUMMARY

X 35 Trench Mortar Battery

(Erase heading not required.)

Place	Date	Hour	Summary of Events and Information	Remarks and references to Appendices
Sheet 24 R.7.a.9.9.	1st to 6th		Battery constructing 6" Trench Mortar Emplacements at N.22.A.45.40 and M.22.a.40.55. - sited to cover reserve line. 3 mortars mounted in position.	ypres
"	7th		Work continued. One other ranks killed by hostile shell fire.	ypres
"	8th to 11th		Work continued.	ypres
Sheet 24 R.21.a.10.80	12th		Handed over positions and mortars to X/30 trench Mortar Battery on relief, and took over 6 mortars situated at R.21.a.10.80. covering second positions. Battery, with exception of detachment for mortars in position, move to billets at Sheet 27 P.23.A.4.5. (near ST SYLVESTRE-CAPPEL).	ypres
"	13th		Nothing to report.	
"	14th		In Corps reserve. Commence training.	ypres
"	15th to 30th		Battery undergoing progressive scheme of training.	ypres
"	31st		The six mortars in position at R.21.a.10.80 withdrawn.	ypres

Ammunition expenditure for the month NIL.
Casualties 1 other rank killed.

J.L. Whitlea, Capt.
Commanding X.35 Trench Mortar Bty.

Army Form C. 2118.

WAR DIARY
or
INTELLIGENCE SUMMARY.
(Erase heading not required.)

Instructions regarding War Diaries and Intelligence Summaries are contained in F. S. Regs., Part II. and the Staff Manual respectively. Title pages will be prepared in manuscript.

Place	Date	Hour	Summary of Events and Information	Remarks and references to Appendices

D. D. & L., London, E.C.

SECRET

WAR DIARY

—of—

Y/35. TRENCH MORTAR BATTERY

FROM 1ST AUGUST TO 31ST AUGUST 1918

Volume 26.

S. Barraclough. Capt. R.F.A.
Commanding Y/35. Trench Mortar Battery

Army Form C. 2118.

WAR DIARY
or
INTELLIGENCE SUMMARY.

(Erase heading not required.)

Instructions regarding War Diaries and Intelligence Summaries are contained in F. S. Regs., Part II. and the Staff Manual respectively. Title pages will be prepared in manuscript.

Place	Date	Hour	Summary of Events and Information	Remarks and references to Appendices

WAR DIARY
INTELLIGENCE SUMMARY

Y/36 Trench Mortar Battery

August 1918

Army Form C. 2118.

Place	Date	Hour	Summary of Events and Information	Remarks and references to Appendices
Sheet 27. R.10.a.9.9.	1st to 6th		Battery constructing 6" trench mortar emplacements at M.21.A.30.12.7 sides to corps reserve line. Two mortars mounted in position.	
"	7th		Work continued. 4 other ranks wounded.	
"	8th to 11th		Work continued.	
"	12th		Handed over positions and mortars to Y/30 Trench Mortar Battery on relief and took over 6 mortars situated at R.10.a.20.40 and R.10.b.90.10., covering second position. Battery, with exception of detachments for mortars in position, move to billets at Sheet 27. P.22.d.99.99. (near ST SYLVESTRE-CAPPEL) working to rehearse.	
	13th		In Corps reserve. Commence training.	
	14th		Battery undergoing progressive scheme of training	
	15th to 30th		The six mortars in position withdrawn.	
	31st		Casualties. Four other ranks wounded. Ammunition expenditure – nil.	

S Hammersley Capt. RHA
Commanding Y/36. Trench Mortar Battery

Army Form C. 2118.

WAR DIARY
or
INTELLIGENCE SUMMARY.
(Erase heading not required.)

Instructions regarding War Diaries and Intelligence Summaries are contained in F. S. Regs., Part II. and the Staff Manual respectively. Title pages will be prepared in manuscript.

Place	Date	Hour	Summary of Events and Information	Remarks and references to Appendices

D.D. & L., London, E.C.
(A10266) Wt. W. 3300/P713 750,000 3/15 Sch. 32 Forms/C2118/16

SECRET.

WAR DIARY

OF

X/35 TRENCH MORTAR BATTERY

FROM 1ST SEPT. 1918 to 30TH SEPT. 1918

Volume 27.

J.G. Whitlaw. Capt.
Commanding X/35. Trench Mortar Battery

Army Form C. 2118.

WAR DIARY
or
INTELLIGENCE SUMMARY.

(*Erase heading not required.*)

Instructions regarding War Diaries and Intelligence Summaries are contained in F.S. Regs., Part II. and the Staff Manual respectively. Title pages will be prepared in manuscript.

Place	Date	Hour	Summary of Events and Information	Remarks and references to Appendices

(A8042) Wt. W1771/M2131 750,000 5/17 Sch. 52 Forms/C2118/14 D. D. & L., London, E.C.

Army Form C. 2118.

WAR DIARY
or
INTELLIGENCE SUMMARY.

(Erase heading not required.)

No. 5. Trench Mortar Battery   September 1918

Instructions regarding War Diaries and Intelligence Summaries are contained in F. S. Regs., Part II. and the Staff Manual respectively. Title pages will be prepared in manuscript.

Place	Date	Hour	Summary of Events and Information	Remarks and references to Appendices
Sheet 27 E.10.a.b.4	1st		Moved to Camp at E.10.a.b.4. Sheet 27.	
do.	2nd to 5th		Nothing to report.	
Sheet 28 H.7.c.7.4	6th		Moved to KNOLLYS FM Camp. H.7.c.7.4. Sheet 28	
	7th		Emplacements reconnoitred for positions for 6" trench mortars. Sites selected at T.31.a.2.0 and at T.32.a.7.5.70. Sheet 28	
	8th		Parties for work on positions moved forward to H.24.B.8.2	
	9th		Work on positions commenced.	
	10th to 14th		Work on positions continued.	
	15th		Work ceases on positions.	
	16th		Reconnaissance for positions for a Field Artillery Brigade.	
	17th 18th 19th		Work on Field Artillery positions continues. Parties employed carrying and stacking ammunition	
	21st 22nd		Moved to HALIFAX CAMP. Party detached to 6 Bty. 157 th Bde R.F.A.	
	28th		Operations commence. Party assists Field Artillery to advance.	
	29th		Nothing to report	
H.24.c.7.5	30th		Moved to H.24.c.7.5. NIL NIL	

Commanding No. 5 Brigade Trench Mortar Battery

Army Form C. 2118.

WAR DIARY
or
INTELLIGENCE SUMMARY.

(*Erase heading not required.*)

Instructions regarding War Diaries and Intelligence Summaries are contained in F. S. Regs., Part II. and the Staff Manual respectively. Title pages will be prepared in manuscript.

Place	Date	Hour	Summary of Events and Information	Remarks and references to Appendices

(A10256) Wt. w. 1300/P713 750,000 2/16 Sch. 52 **Forms/C2118/16**
D. D. & L., London, E.C.

SECRET

WAR DIARY

OF

Y/35 TRENCH MORTAR BATTERY

FROM. 1ST SEPT 1918 TO 30TH SEPT. 1918

Volume 27

H. Ritchie
Lieut R.F.A.
for. O.C. Y/35. Trench Mortar Battery

Army Form C. 2118.

WAR DIARY
or
INTELLIGENCE SUMMARY.
(Erase heading not required.)

Instructions regarding War Diaries and Intelligence Summaries are contained in F. S. Regs., Part II. and the Staff Manual respectively. Title pages will be prepared in manuscript.

Place	Date	Hour	Summary of Events and Information	Remarks and references to Appendices

D. D. & L., London, E.C.
(A804) Wt. W1771/M2731 730,000 5/17 Sch. 52 Forms/C2118/14

WAR DIARY
or
INTELLIGENCE SUMMARY.

Army Form C. 2118.

V/35 Trench Mortar Battery   September 1918

(Erase heading not required.)

Instructions regarding War Diaries and Intelligence Summaries are contained in F. S. Regs., Part II. and the Staff Manual respectively. Title pages will be prepared in manuscript.

Place	Date	Hour	Summary of Events and Information	Remarks and references to Appendices
Shell 24 E.10.c.5.h	1st		Moved to Camp at E.10.a.6.4. Sheet 27. MM	
— " —	2nd (3rd ?)	2am (6 c'gh?)	Nothing to report. MM	
Sheet 28 H.7.c.7.4	6th		Moved to KNOLLYS F.M. Camp H.7.c.7. Sheet 28. MM to reconnoitre front reconnoitered for position for 6" heavy mortars	
— " —	7th		Nothing to report. MM	
— " —	8th		Party of 20 men attached to B/139 Brigade R.F.A. to assist in construction of wagon lines. MM	
— " —	9th			
— " —	10th to 13th incl		Remainder of battery employed on camp fatigues. MM	
— " —	14th		Work on positions for a Field Artillery Brigade commenced. MM	
— " —	15th 16th (to 25th?)		Work on positions and ammunition stacking continues. MM	
— " —	27th		Work completed. Party of 18 attached to 139 Bde R.F.A. MM	
— " —	28th		Operations commenced. Party assists field artillery to advance. MM	
— " —	29th		Nothing to report. MM	
H.24.c.7.5	30th		Moved to H.24.c.7.5. MM	

W. Mitchell Lieut.
Commanding V/35 Trench Mortar Battery

Casualties

Ammunition Expenditure NIL
                        NIL

Army Form C. 2118.

WAR DIARY

or

INTELLIGENCE SUMMARY.

(Erase heading not required.)

Instructions regarding War Diaries and Intelligence Summaries are contained in F. S. Regs., Part II. and the Staff Manual respectively. Title pages will be prepared in manuscript.

Place	Date	Hour	Summary of Events and Information	Remarks and references to Appendices

(A10256) Wt. W. 13090/P713 750,000 9/15 Sch. 52 Forms/C2118/16 D. D. & L., London, E.C.

SECRET

WAR DIARY

of

X/35 TRENCH MORTAR BATTERY

FROM 1ST OCTO TO 31ST OCTO 1918

VOLUME 28

J. W. L. Ship   Capt
Commanding X/35. Trench Mortar Battery

WAR DIARY
or
INTELLIGENCE SUMMARY.

(Erase heading not required.)

Army Form C. 2118.

Instructions regarding War Diaries and Intelligence Summaries are contained in F. S. Regs., Part II and the Staff Manual respectively. Title pages will be prepared in manuscript.

Place	Date	Hour	Summary of Events and Information	Remarks and references to Appendices

Army Form C. 2118.

X/35. Trench Mortar Battery   October 1918

WAR DIARY
or
INTELLIGENCE SUMMARY
(Erase heading not required.)

Instructions regarding War Diaries and Intelligence
Summaries are contained in F. S. Regs., Part II.
and the Staff Manual respectively. Title pages
will be prepared in manuscript.

Place	Date	Hour	Summary of Events and Information	Remarks and references to Appendices
Sheet 28 H.2.4.b.7.5	1st.		Battery employed as working parties on to rest ammunition dumps and in salving captured enemy guns.	
"	2nd. to 13th.		Work on ammunition dumps, and salving continued.	
"	14th.		Three signallers detached to H.headquarters. 35th Divl. Arty for duty	
"	15th. to 16th.		Work on ammunition dumps continued	
"	17th.		moved to L.14.c.7.5. Sheet 28., and commenced work on Ammunition Refilling Point.	
"	18th.		Work continued. 2nd Lt. H. PLAYLE. R.F.A (attached 157th Brigade R.F.A)	
"	19th.		Work continued. wounded in action	
BISSEGHEM.	20th		moved to BISSEGHEM. G.35.A.7.7. Sheet 29, Refilling Point. One carriage for 6" mobile Ammunition trench mortar Canadian Corps. pattern received from Ordnance	
"	21st to 23rd.		Work on Refilling Point continued	
"	24th		Work on dumps ceased. Commenced training on the mobile mortar.	
"	25th		Mobile mortar with detachment and teams under charge of Lt. R.F. SPALDING attached to 159th Brigade. R.F.A. One further mobile	

Army Form C. 2118.

WAR DIARY
or
INTELLIGENCE SUMMARY.

(Erase heading not required.)

Instructions regarding War Diaries and Intelligence Summaries are contained in F. S. Regs., Part II. and the Staff Manual respectively. Title pages will be prepared in manuscript.

Place	Date	Hour	Summary of Events and Information	Remarks and references to Appendices
BISSEGHEM	26th		Carriage received from Ordnance. Training on mobile trench mortar continued. Fired 20 rounds experimental	
SWEVEGHEM O.2.b.8.3. Sheet 29.	27th		Training on mobile trench mortar continued.	
	28th		Moved to Sweveghem O.2.b.8.3. Salving of enemy guns continued.	
	29.		Salved two enemy 77 guns & one 5.9 Howitzer.	
	30		Fired 40 rounds from mobile mortar at P.29.c.5.2. Reconnoitred and found positions for 6" T. Mortar.	
	31		Two 6" mortars in action.	
			Fired 12 rounds in support of operation. Target approached to RUSSE P.29.d. during 1/4hr	

A.E. Whitham Capt.
Commanding X/35 Trench Mortar Battery.

Army Form C. 2118.

WAR DIARY
or
INTELLIGENCE SUMMARY.

(Erase heading not required.)

Place	Date	Hour	Summary of Events and Information	Remarks and references to Appendices

Instructions regarding War Diaries and Intelligence Summaries are contained in F. S. Regs., Part II. and the Staff Manual respectively. Title pages will be prepared in manuscript.

SECRET

WAR DIARY

of

Y/35 TRENCH MORTAR BATTERY

FROM 1ST OCT° TO 31ST OCT° 1918

VOLUME 28

S. Barraclough Capt.
Commanding Y/35 Trench Mortar Battery

Army Form C. 2118.

WAR DIARY
or
INTELLIGENCE SUMMARY.
(Erase heading not required.)

X39 TRENCH MORTAR BATTERY

of

ANZAC DIVSY

Place	Date	Hour	Summary of Events and Information	Remarks and references to Appendices

Instructions regarding War Diaries and Intelligence Summaries are contained in F.S. Regs., Part II. and the Staff Manual respectively. Title pages will be prepared in manuscript.

WAR DIARY / INTELLIGENCE SUMMARY

1/5th Trench Mortar Battery

October 1918

Army Form C. 2118.

Place	Date	Hour	Summary of Events and Information	Remarks and references to Appendices
Sheet 28 H.24.b.7.5.	1st		Battery employed as working parties on road and in salving captured enemy guns.	S.S
"	2nd to 13th		Work on ammunition dumps, Ammunition Dumps and salving continued.	S.S
"	14th		Three signallers detached to Headquarters 35th Mid Arty for duty. Lt. H.M. MICHIE. R.F.A. attached to the 104th Infantry Brigade for duty as artillery liaison Officer during our advance.	S.S
"	15th to 16th		Work on ammunition dumps continued.	S.S
Sheet 28. L.14.c.7.5	19th		Moved to L.14.c.7.5. Sheet 28. and commenced work on Ammunition Refilling point.	S.S
"	18th to 22nd		Work continued	S.S
BISSEGHEM.	23rd		Moved to BISSEGHEM. G.35.A.7.7. Sheet 29.	S.S
	24th		Worked on ammunition dump	S.S
	25th		Two carriages for 6" mobile mortars to another Corps portion received from Ordnance. Training on mobile mortar continues	S.S
SWEVEGHEM.	26th		Moves to Sweveghem at O.2.d.8.3. Salving of captured enemy guns and ammunition continued.	S.S
	27th			S.S

Army Form C. 2118.

WAR DIARY
or
INTELLIGENCE SUMMARY
(Erase heading not required.)

Instructions regarding War Diaries and Intelligence Summaries are contained in F. S. Regs., Part II. and the Staff Manual respectively. Title pages will be prepared in manuscript.

Place	Date	Hour	Summary of Events and Information	Remarks and references to Appendices
SWEVEGHEM	28th		One captured 105 m.m. How. with detachments and limber under Li. H. L. Finicken attached to 159 Brigade R.F.A.	S.B.
	29th		Reconnoitred and found position for 6" T.M. at P.28.	S.B.
	30th		2 mortars in action a P.28.	S.B.
	31st		Fired 19 rounds in support of operations. Target approaches to RUGGE Pog d. Shot 29.	S.B.

S Banabugh Capt: R.F.A.
Commanding Y/35th S. Mortar Battery.

Army Form C. 2118.

WAR DIARY
or
INTELLIGENCE SUMMARY.

(Erase heading not required.)

Instructions regarding War Diaries and Intelligence Summaries are contained in F. S. Regs., Part II. and the Staff Manual respectively. Title pages will be prepared in manuscript.

Place	Date	Hour	Summary of Events and Information	Remarks and references to Appendices

SECRET.

WAR DIARY

of

X/35 TRENCH MORTAR BATTERY

FROM 1st NOV. 1918 to 30th NOV 1918

VOLUME 29

J. G. Whitham Capt.
Commanding X/35 Trench Mortar Battery

WAR DIARY
or
INTELLIGENCE SUMMARY.

(Erase heading not required.)

Army Form C. 2118.

Instructions regarding War Diaries and Intelligence Summaries are contained in F. S. Regs., Part II. and the Staff Manual respectively. Title pages will be prepared in manuscript.

Place	Date	Hour	Summary of Events and Information	Remarks and references to Appendices

WAR DIARY or INTELLIGENCE SUMMARY

Army Form C. 2118.

N/45 Trench Mortar Battery   November 1918

Place	Date	Hour	Summary of Events and Information	Remarks and references to Appendices
Sheet 29 O.2, P.8.3	1st		Trench mortars withdrawn from action; 3 mortars limbering up	
			Mobile Trench Mortars	
"	2nd (a)		Training continues	
	3rd			
	4th (?)		Training continues	
	5th			
"	6th		Horse transport (11 lorries, 23 mules, 2 G.S. wagons) arrived on attachment from 35th D.A.C. to commence the two mobile mortars. Four mortars limbered up	
"	7th		Moved forward to Ooteghem	
"	8th	9 AM	Moved on mobile mortars continues	
Sheet 29 P.3.A.c.7	9th		Battery with mobile mortars attached to 157th the Bde R.F.A. at P.3.A.c.7. (Sheet 29)	
X.A.C.6.4	10th	10 AM	Advanced with 157th Bde R.F.A. to X.A.C.6.4. (Sheet 29)	
R.33.a.8.9	11th	11.00 hrs	Hostilities cease 11.00 hrs. Battery moved to R.33.A.8.9. (Sheet 29)	
"	12th		Nothing to report	
Q.24.a.S.5	13th		Moved to Q.24.a.5.5. (Sheet 29)	
BERGHEM	14th		Moved to BERGHEM (Q.21.d. Sheet 29)	
"	15th		Nothing to report	
	to 16th			
CUERNE	17th		Moved to billets in CUERNE (R.10.a. Sheet 29)	

WAR DIARY
or
INTELLIGENCE SUMMARY.

Army Form C. 2118.

Place	Date	Hour	Summary of Events and Information	Remarks and references to Appendices
CUERNE	18/11 onwards		Battery undergoing training and overhauling material and equipment.	
MENIN	30.11		Moved to MENIN. Ammunition expenditure for the month NIL — Casualties — Nil	

J.R. Luther
Major
Commanding X 50. Trench Mortar Battery

Army Form C. 2118.

WAR DIARY

or

INTELLIGENCE SUMMARY.

(Erase heading not required.)

Instructions regarding War Diaries and Intelligence Summaries are contained in F. S. Regs., Part II. and the Staff Manual respectively. Title pages will be prepared in manuscript.

Place	Date	Hour	Summary of Events and Information	Remarks and references to Appendices

D. D. & L., London, E.C.
(A10560) W\. \ 1300/P713 750,000 7/15 Sch. 52 Forms/C2118/16

SECRET.

WAR DIARY
of
Y/35 TRENCH MORTAR BATTERY

FROM 1st NOV 1918 TO 30th NOV. 1918.

VOLUME 29

C. A. Harris Lieut
Commanding Y/35. Trench Mortar Battery

Army Form C. 2118.

WAR DIARY
or
INTELLIGENCE SUMMARY.
(Erase heading not required.)

Place	Date	Hour	Summary of Events and Information	Remarks and references to Appendices

Instructions regarding War Diaries and Intelligence Summaries are contained in F. S. Regs., Part II. and the Staff Manual respectively. Title pages will be prepared in manuscript.

Army Form C. 2118.

WAR DIARY
or
INTELLIGENCE SUMMARY.

(Erase heading not required.)

Unit: 4/5 Seven Inches Battery   Month: November 1918

Instructions regarding War Diaries and Intelligence Summaries are contained in F.S. Regs., Part II. and the Staff Manual respectively. Title pages will be prepared in manuscript.

Place	Date	Hour	Summary of Events and Information	Remarks and references to Appendices
Sheet 29 O.2.b.8.3	1st		Sent mortar withdrawn from action. To commence training on mobile trench mortars.	Copy
"	2nd (& 5th)		Training continued	Copy
"	6th		Some transport (11 horses, 2 mules, 2 G.S. and 1 G.S. wagon) arrived on attachment from 5 in. R.B.E. to complete the two mobile mortars. Four mortars complete with stores returned to Ordnance.	Copy
"	7th & 8th		Training on mobile mortars continued	Copy
Sheet 29 P.10.c.2.2.	9th		Battery with mobile mortars attaches to 159th Bde R.F.A. at 26.2.22 Sheet 29	Copy
AUDENHOVE	10th		Moved with 159th Bde to AUDENHOVE (N.3.a Sheet 30)	Copy
Sheet 30 O.31.a.3.3	11th		Moved to O.31.a.3.3 (Sheet 30) reconnaissances made N.I.29.	Copy
Sheet 29 R.33.a.8.9	12th		Moved to R.33.a.8.9 (Sheet 29)	Copy
Sheet 30 Q.24.a.5.5	13th		Moved to Q.24.a.5.5 (Sheet 29)	Copy
Sheet 30 Q.21.d.	14th		Moved to BERCHEM (Q.21.d. Sheet 29)	Copy
	15th 30th		Nothing to report.	Copy

Army Form C. 2118.

WAR DIARY
or
INTELLIGENCE SUMMARY.
(Erase heading not required.)

Place	Date	Hour	Summary of Events and Information	Remarks and references to Appendices
SUERNE			Moved to billets at SUERNE (Sheet 20)	Copy
	14.2.17 onward		Daily musquetry training and maintaining moving requirements	Copy
MENIN	30.4.17		Moved to MENIN	Copy
			Conversion diversion to the montaines	
			Casualties - Nil.	

Castens [sig]
Commanding 1/22 ...

Army Form C. 2118.

WAR DIARY
or
INTELLIGENCE SUMMARY.

(Erase heading not required.)

Place	Date	Hour	Summary of Events and Information	Remarks and references to Appendices

Instructions regarding War Diaries and Intelligence Summaries are contained in F.S. Regs. Part II. and the Staff Manual respectively. Title pages will be prepared in manuscript.

SECRET.

WAR DIARY
OF
X/35 TRENCH MORTAR BATTERY.

FROM 1ST DEC. 1918 TO 31ST DEC. 1918

VOLUME 30

C.W. Pickford. Captain R.F.A.
для Officer Commanding X/35. Trench Mortar Battery

Army Form C. 2118.

WAR DIARY
or
INTELLIGENCE SUMMARY.
(Erase heading not required.)

X 92 TRENCH MORTAR BATTERY.

from 21st to 31st DEC 1918.

Place	Date	Hour	Summary of Events and Information	Remarks and references to Appendices

Instructions regarding War Diaries and Intelligence Summaries are contained in F. S. Regs., Part II. and the Staff Manual respectively. Title pages will be prepared in manuscript.

Army Form C. 2118.

X/55 Trench Mortar Battery   WAR DIARY   December 1918
                                    or
                           INTELLIGENCE SUMMARY.
(Erase heading not required.)

Instructions regarding War Diaries and Intelligence Summaries are contained in F. S. Regs., Part II. and the Staff Manual respectively. Title pages will be prepared in manuscript.

Place	Date	Hour	Summary of Events and Information	Remarks and references to Appendices
POPERINGHE	1st.		Battery on line of march moved from MENIN to HAMILTON CAMP. near POPERINGHE	
TERDEGHEM	2nd.		Moved to TERDEGHEM	
NIEURLET	3rd.		Moved to NIEURLET	
" "	4th.		Nothing to report.	
ST MOMELIN	5th.		Moved to billets in ST MOMELIN.	
"	6th to 24th		Battery in training. Educational classes commenced in accordance with G.H.Q. educational scheme.	
"	25th to 30th		Commenced retiring in the area G.20, 26 and 21 (Sheet 24)	

A.W. Phelps
Capt. R.F.A.
p/officer Commanding X/55 Trench Mortar Battery

Army Form C. 2118.

WAR DIARY
or
INTELLIGENCE SUMMARY.
(Erase heading not required.)

Instructions regarding War Diaries and Intelligence Summaries are contained in F. S. Regs., Part II. and the Staff Manual respectively. Title pages will be prepared in manuscript.

Place	Date	Hour	Summary of Events and Information	Remarks and references to Appendices

(A8004) D. D. & L., London, E.C. Wt. W1771/M271 750,000 5/17 **Sch. 32** Forms/C2118/14

SECRET.

WAR DIARY

OF

Y/35 TRENCH MORTAR BATTERY.

FROM 1ST DEC. 1918. TO 31ST DEC. 1918.

VOLUME 30

S. Barraclough. Captain R.F.A.
Commanding Y/35. Trench Mortar Battery.

Army Form C. 2118.

WAR DIARY
or
INTELLIGENCE SUMMARY.
(Erase heading not required.)

Instructions regarding War Diaries and Intelligence Summaries are contained in F. S. Regs., Part II. and the Staff Manual respectively. Title pages will be prepared in manuscript.

Place	Date	Hour	Summary of Events and Information	Remarks and references to Appendices

D. D. & L., London, E.C.
(A8004) Wt. W.2771/M2-31 750,000 5/17 Sch. 52 Forms/C2118/14

WAR DIARY Y/85 Trench Mortar Battery November 1918 Army Form C. 2118.

Place	Date	Hour	Summary of Events and Information	Remarks and references to Appendices
POPERINGHE	1st		Battery on line on march, moved from MENIN to HAMILTON CAMP near POPERINGHE	SF
TERDEGHEM	2nd		moved to TERDEGHEM	SF
NIEURLET	3rd		moved to NIEURLET	SF
"	4th		nothing to report. Lt. H. MICHIE R.F.A. posted to 159th Bde R.F.A.	SF
ST MOMELIN	5th		moved to billets in ST. MOMELIN	SF
"	6th to 19th		Battery in training. Educational classes commenced in accordance with G.H.Q. educational scheme	SF
"	20th to 30th		Commenced salvage in the area G.20. 25 and 26 (Sheet 27)	SF

Barraclough Capt. R.F.A.
Commanding Y/85 Trench Mortar Battery

Army Form C. 2118.

WAR DIARY
or
INTELLIGENCE SUMMARY.
(Erase heading not required.)

Instructions regarding War Diaries and Intelligence Summaries are contained in F. S. Regs., Part II. and the Staff Manual respectively. Title pages will be prepared in manuscript.

Place	Date	Hour	Summary of Events and Information	Remarks and references to Appendices

SECRET

WAR DIARY

X/35 TRENCH MORTAR BATTERY

FROM 1ST JAN 1919 to 31ST JAN 1919.

VOLUME 31.

[signature] Capt. R.F.A.
for O/C X/35 Trench Mortar Battery

INTELLIGENCE SUMMARY.

(Erase heading not required.)

Instructions regarding War Diaries and Intelligence Summaries are contained in F. S. Regs., Part II. and the Staff Manual respectively. Title pages will be prepared in manuscript.

Place	Date	Hour	Summary of Events and Information	Remarks and references to Appendices

INTELLIGENCE SUMMARY.

(Erase heading not required.)

Place	Date	Hour	Summary of Events and Information	Remarks and references to Appendices
St. Momelin	1st 4th		Education Classes continued in accordance with 9.H.Q. Col. Scheme. Saving continued. area 9.2.0.2.S and 26. (Sheet 27)	S/S
	8th		Saving and Educational Classes continued. 1.O.R. proceeded for dispersal. (Watford Detail. area 10.A.)	S/S
	9th		Nothing to report.	S/S
	10th		Saving and Education Classes continued. LT. R.F SPALDING. R.F.A. proceeded on course. XIX Corps Schools. 2.O.Rs proceeded for dispersal. (area. 8 and 10.A.)	S/S
	11th		Saving and Education Classes continued. 2/LT. A.G.K.S. JONES. and 2.O.Rs proceeded for dispersal. (area. 2.B.)	S/S
	12th		Saving and Education Classes continued. 2.O.Rs proceeded for dispersal (area 4.B.)	S/S
	13th 15th		Saving and Education Classes continued.	S/S
	16th		Nothing to report.	S/S

Army Form C. 2118.

WAR DIARY
or
INTELLIGENCE SUMMARY.

(Erase heading not required.)

X/35 Infty   January 1919

Instructions regarding War Diaries and Intelligence Summaries are contained in F. S. Regs., Part II. and the Staff Manual respectively. Title pages will be prepared in manuscript.

Place	Date	Hour	Summary of Events and Information	Remarks and references to Appendices
St. Pomelin	14th		Salving and Education Classes continued. 2 O.R.s proceeded for dispersal. (area 6.B.) 3 O.R.s leave to U.K. via Calais 15.1.19 till 31.1.19.	SD
	18th		Salving and Education Classes continued. 1 O.R. proceeds of for dispersal. (area 8.)	SD
	19th		Salving and Education Classes continued. 1 O.R. proceeded for dispersal. (area 8.B.)	SD
	20th		Salving and Education Classes continued. 1 O.R. proceeded for dispersal. (area 9.B.)	SD
	21st		Salving and Education Classes continued. 2 O.R. proceeded for dispersal. (area 4.A.) 1 O.R. leave to United K. via Calais 22.1.19 till 4.2.19. 3 O.R.s returned from Course. N⁰ 4. Ordnance Mobile Workshops. (Heavy.)	SD
	22nd		1. O.R. proceeded on Course. XIX Corps Schools. Salving and Education Classes continued.	SD
	23rd		Salving and Education Classes continued.	SD

WAR DIARY
or
INTELLIGENCE SUMMARY.

(Erase heading not required.)

X/35 JMB4

Instructions regarding War Diaries and Intelligence Summaries are contained in F. S. Regs., Part II. and the Staff Manual respectively. Title pages will be prepared in manuscript.

Place	Date	Hour	Summary of Events and Information	Remarks and references to Appendices
St. Momlin	24th		Salving and Education Classes continued. 1 O.R. Leave to U.K. via Calais. 25.1.19 till 8.2.19. 1 O.R. proceeded for dispersal. (area S.A.)	SL
	25th		Salving and Education Classes continued.	SL
	26th		2. O.R.s proceeded for dispersal. (area 2.B.)	SL
	27th		Salving and Education Classes continued. 1 O.R. proceeded for dispersal. (area 6.B.)	SL
	28th		Salving and Education Classes continued. 1 O.R. Leave to U.K. via Calais.	SL
	29th		Salving and Education Classes continued.	SL
	30th			
	31st		Salving and Education Classes continued. 4 O.R.s proceeded for dispersal. (area.3.)	SL

S. Stanley

C.R.A. 33rd DIVISION

WAR DIARY
or
INTELLIGENCE SUMMARY.

(Erase heading not required.)

Instructions regarding War Diaries and Intelligence Summaries are contained in F. S. Regs., Part II. and the Staff Manual respectively. Title pages will be prepared in manuscript.

Place	Date	Hour	Summary of Events and Information	Remarks and references to Appendices

SECRET

WAR DIARY

Y/35 TRENCH MORTAR BATTERY

FROM 1st JAN 1919 to 31st JAN 1919

VOLUME 31

Capt R.F.A
O.C. Y/35 Trench Mortar Battery

WAR DIARY
or
INTELLIGENCE SUMMARY.

(Erase heading not required.)

Instructions regarding War Diaries and Intelligence Summaries are contained in F. S. Regs., Part II. and the Staff Manual respectively. Title pages will be prepared in manuscript.

Place	Date	Hour	Summary of Events and Information	Remarks and references to Appendices

INTELLIGENCE SUMMARY.

(Erase heading not required.)

Place	Date	Hour	Summary of Events and Information	Remarks and references to Appendices
St. Martin	1st		Education Classes continued in accordance with G.H.Q. Ed. Scheme.	SB
	3rd		Salving continued. area 9.20. 25" and 26. (Sheet 24.)	SB
	4th		Salving and Education Classes continued. 1 O.R. proceeded for dispersal (area 3.)	SB
	5th – 9th		Education Classes and Salving continued.	SB
	10th		Salving and Education Classes continued. 2 O.R. proceeded for dispersal (area 5.B.)	SB
	11th		Salving and Education Classes continued. 1 O.R. proceeded for dispersal. (area 9.B.)	SB
	12th		Salving and Education Classes continued. 1 O.R. proceeded for dispersal. (area 2.A.)	SB
	13th – 18th		Salving and Education Classes continued.	SB
	19th		1 O.R. proceeded for dispersal. (area 10.A.) 1 OFFR Leave to U.K. via Calais. 20.1.19. till 2.2.19.	SB
	20th		Salving and Education Classes continued. 2 O.R.s Leave to U.K. via Calais. 21.1.19. till 3.2.19.	SB

S. Shackleton

INTELLIGENCE SUMMARY.

(Erase heading not required.)

Place	Date	Hour	Summary of Events and Information	Remarks and references to Appendices
St. Momelin	21st		Salving and Education Classes continued. 8 O.Rs proceeded for dispersal. (area 10.A.) 1 O.R. returned from France. No. 4 Mobile Workshop Ordnance. (Heavy.)	SD
	22nd		Salving and Education Classes continued. Lieut. C.A. Harris. Gloug. Reg.M.T. and 1 O.R. proceeded for dispersal. (area 10.A.)	SD
	23rd		Salving and Education Classes continued.	SD
	24th		Salving and Education Classes continued. 2.O.Rs proceeded for dispersal. (area 10.A.)	SD
	25th		Salving and Education Classes continued.	SD
	26th		Nothing to report.	SD
	27th–30th		Salving and Education Classes continued.	SD
	31st		Salving and Education Classes continued. 3 O.Rs proceeded for dispersal. (area 5 B.)	SD

S. Sanadough
CAPT., R.F.A.
D.E.M.O., 35th DIVISION

Army Form C. 2118.

WAR DIARY
or
INTELLIGENCE SUMMARY.

(Erase heading not required.)

Instructions regarding War Diaries and Intelligence Summaries are contained in F. S. Regs., Part II. and the Staff Manual respectively. Title pages will be prepared in manuscript.

Place	Date	Hour	Summary of Events and Information	Remarks and references to Appendices

D.D. & L., London, E.C.
(A10260) Wt. W. 5300/P713 750,000 8/15 Sch. 32 Forms/C2118/16

www.ingramcontent.com/pod-product-compliance
Lightning Source LLC
Chambersburg PA
CBHW080911230426

43667CB00015B/2651